Praise for
Firsthand

"It's rare to find young people unafraid to voice their doubts while still being bold in their faith. Ryan and Josh are two of those people."

> —MARK BATTERSON, lead pastor of National Community Church, Washington, DC, and author of the *New York Times* bestseller *The Circle Maker*

"Josh and Ryan Shook, the sons of well-known pastor and author Kerry Shook, have fully embraced the fact that although their dad gave them a great start, they need to run their own race. Learn how to embrace a firsthand faith and walk in the strength of a personal relationship with Christ."

> —STEVEN FURTICK, lead pastor of Elevation Church, Charlotte, NC, and author of the *New York Times* bestseller *Greater*

"*Firsthand* is a rich and insightful book for believers who are tired of secondhand religion. In this honest, compelling, and well-written book, Ryan Shook and Josh Shook have given us a huge gift! Their candor is so refreshing, and they point the way to a vibrant, personal faith. This could be one of the most important books you'll ever read."

> —JUD WILHITE, senior pastor of Central Christian Church, Las Vegas, NV, and author of *Pursued*

"All Christian parents want their children to develop a faith of their own. *Firsthand* asks tough questions and guides those with a secondhand faith to find Christ for themselves."

—CRAIG GROESCHEL, pastor of LifeChurch.tv, Edmond, OK, and author of *Soul Detox*

"Ryan and Josh Shook don't shy away from the tough questions but face them head-on in this powerful book that will encourage young adults not to settle for an inherited faith but to discover a true relationship with Jesus that is unique, exciting, and every bit their own."

—PETE WILSON, pastor of Cross Point Church, Nashville, TN, and author of *Plan B*

"*Firsthand* is an honest and powerful book that will help readers find their own identities through Jesus Christ. Far too often the gospel is experienced secondhand, and the importance of a personal relationship with God goes overlooked. Ryan and Josh Shook provide very detailed lessons that have helped them grow in their own faith, and they are sure to provide a breath of fresh air to anyone else. *Firsthand* will empower readers to define their own experience with God, and I would recommend it to believers new and old."

—MATTHEW BARNETT, senior pastor of Angelus Temple and the Dream Center, Los Angeles, CA, and author of *The Church That Never Sleeps*

"You can't live a purpose-driven life without a real and personal faith. Christ didn't come to start a religion; he came to connect with you in a genuine firsthand relationship. Ryan and Josh Shook will challenge you never to settle for a secondhand religion but instead to develop a personal faith that transforms your life."

—RICK WARREN, founding pastor of Saddleback Church, Lake Forest, CA, and author of the *New York Times* #1 bestseller *The Purpose Driven Life*

firsthand
Ryan & Josh Shook

Ditching Secondhand Religion
for a Faith of Your Own

WATERBROOK
PRESS

FIRSTHAND
PUBLISHED BY WATERBROOK PRESS
12265 Oracle Boulevard, Suite 200
Colorado Springs, Colorado 80921

Unless otherwise noted, individuals' comments came from online surveys conducted on September 4 and September 18, 2012, specifically for this book.

Details in some anecdotes and stories have been changed to protect the identities of the persons involved.

ISBN 978-0-307-88629-3
ISBN 978-0-307-88630-9 (electronic)

Published in the United States by WaterBrook Multnomah, an imprint of the Crown Publishing Group, a division of Random House Inc., New York.

WATERBROOK and its deer colophon are registered trademarks of Random House Inc.

Cataloging-in-Publication Data is on file with the Library of Congress.

Printed in the United States of America
2013

10 9 8 7 6 5 4 3

SPECIAL SALES
Most WaterBrook Multnomah books are available at special quantity discounts when purchased in bulk by corporations, organizations, and special-interest groups. Custom imprinting or excerpting can also be done to fit special needs. For information, please e-mail SpecialMarkets@WaterBrookMultnomah.com or call 1-800-603-7051.

Contents

Why Firsthand Matters
A Faith Straight from the Source

There comes a time when you can no
longer cling to your parents' coattails
and you have to choose to make it
your faith.

—Robert Griffin III

I admit I once lived by rumors of you;
now I have it all firsthand.

—Job 42:5 (MSG)

Hi, we're Ryan and Josh Shook, two brothers in our twenties.

We've met before, actually. You see, even though you've probably never met us personally, you know people just like us. You've known them at every church you've attended. We've been on your football team, gone to the same parties, been in your group of friends.

You took one look at us and thought, *They're such good Christians.* But you saw us when we were at our best. We were the leaders of the youth group, and you thought we probably had it all together.

So how could we possibly relate to you?

The truth is, we've both come back from the brink of spiritual death. Really. Only a short time ago we were so done with the whole Christian thing. Whatever we looked like on the outside, inside we were desperate for something more. Nothing at church satisfied the inner hunger gnawing at us. Being a Christian seemed to be only about going through the motions, following rules, keeping up appearances.

So we tried something else. We lived as if God didn't exist. That worked for a while. And then it eventually stopped working. Actually, we ended up feeling even more desperate and unfulfilled than before.

Maybe you know what we're talking about. Maybe you've given up on church and its promise of contentment. Maybe you've not only given up on church but given up on God as well. Or maybe you're just now starting to suspect that something is wrong but you can't put your finger on it.

If any of these scenarios apply to you, you're not alone.

The truth is, between the ages of sixteen and twenty-six, most young people experience a crisis of faith. Suddenly the beliefs that made sense yesterday are no longer relevant today. Our faith feels flimsy and fake.

For us it felt something like this: We had traveled halfway across a bridge and couldn't get any further. The bridge just ended. On the riverbank behind us, we could see the Christianity that worked when we were younger. Ahead of us, on the opposite bank, we could see, well, not much really. Mostly fog.

That didn't feel good.

As it turns out, our experience is common for kids who grew up in church. David Kinnaman, president of the Barna Group, a research and resource organization, investigated our generation's dissatisfaction with traditional Christianity for his book *You Lost Me*. "The problem," Kinnaman tells us, "is not that this generation has been less churched than children and teens before them; the problem is that much spiritual energy fades away during a crucial decade of life—the twenties."[1]

We had traveled halfway across a bridge and couldn't get any further. The bridge just ended.

Spiritual energy fades away. That description resonates deeply with us. After years of going to church, following the rules, and trying to replicate the faith of our parents, we had to admit that something was fading fast in our souls.

But there's good news.

Right in the middle of our personal crises, we made a discovery that changed everything.

No Point Pretending

What we discovered was that what we *thought* was our faith wasn't ours after all. Not completely. Mostly it belonged to our parents. Some of it belonged to the youth pastor or our friends. Sure, some of it was real for us too. But a lot of it wasn't. If you had closely inspected our personal beliefs, you might have noticed some flimsy plastic labels hanging on them.

On them would have been scribbled "Secondhand."

Or maybe "Belongs to Dad."

Or "Just trying to fit in."

Our faith was something we had inherited, and it felt like it was not originally intended for us. That wasn't our parents' fault. Or the youth pastor's. Or the church's.

Our parents taught us that Christianity wasn't about religion and rules but about a relationship with the God who made us. Yes, they made mistakes. But we saw them live out a genuine faith in front of us—two imperfect parents seeking to trust a perfect God. We truly feel blessed to have parents who have a real and authentic faith. But it's *theirs*.

It doesn't matter how real your parents' faith is, or anyone else's for that matter, if you don't develop a faith of your own. A handed-down faith that you've never owned for yourself doesn't give meaning to your life. You might sort of wear it, but it doesn't say much about who you are. In fact, hand-me-down beliefs can start to weigh on you. They become a source of shame and guilt, a bar set too high that reminds you of your failures. Or they just seem outdated and irrelevant.

Hand-me-down faith may work when things are going well, but when pressures and problems hit, what you thought you believed will crumble.

"I hate to say this, but so many of the so-called Christian kids on this campus really turn me off," Taylor, a university sophomore on the West Coast, told us. "The guys from church party just like the rest. At the frat parties they just want to get the girls drunk so that they can get their clothes off. They say they're Christians—but come on!" That kind of faith is more like a shirt you wear when you're with a certain group of friends. In reality, that kind of faith is not faith at all! It's secondhand religion, and it doesn't get inside your life or change anything about you.

Mike, a university senior we read about, was at least more honest than those frat guys. He told an interviewer he had grown up going to church and learning about God, but in college he wasn't so sure anymore that God even existed. Mike was looking for solid evidence that God is real. He said that during his search he felt like he was an "adopted child wanting to know the truth about [my] birth parents."[2]

We think Mike is right not to rely completely on the faith of his parents just because they are his parents. If you don't believe in God because of your own convictions, there is no point in pretending that you believe at all.

If you don't believe in God because of your own convictions, there is no point in pretending that you believe at all.

Firsthand faith *is not* something you wear on the outside. Firsthand faith, in our experience, is centered deep in your own mind and heart. Sure, it's still a work in progress, but it's *yours*. It's *you*. When hard times hit, you have a lot to draw on to weather the storm. In fact, firsthand faith is so real and personal that it just gets stronger when it is challenged.

Who wouldn't want that kind of living, breathing faith?

That is why our goal in writing this book is to help you replace secondhand religion with a faith—and most important, a relationship—that is meaningful. We want to help you get from a religion you wear on the outside when it's convenient to a faith of your own—one that's authentically yours all the way through.

YOU CAN BEAT THE ODDS

We have spent the past few years talking with friends and doing research, trying to get to the heart of what it means to seek and experience a genuine Christian faith for ourselves. We even conducted a survey with about three hundred strangers of different ages to get their views. Some of the people we got in touch with have traded in their secondhand faith for a firsthand faith. Others are still in the midst of the struggle, and who knows where they're going to come out in the end? You'll hear some of their voices, along with ours, in the course of this book.

Frankly, it wasn't hard at all to find people who have been through a crisis in their faith, just as we have.

One research study showed that about 60 percent of young people who were active in church as teenagers failed to translate that into an active spiritual commitment during their early adulthood.[3] That's a whole lot of people who discovered that a secondhand faith didn't get them very far. When adult life with all its possibilities called out to them, they found that following God didn't really matter much to them anymore.

As we were writing this book, another study came out showing that while 89 percent of high schoolers claim to be affiliated with some religion in some way, the number drops to 75 percent once they get into their twenties.[4] Even among those people who still consider themselves Christians, nearly two-thirds of college students and three-quarters of those who don't attend college cut way back on their church involvement after they cross the threshold of high school graduation.[5]

The statistics about younger Christians who don't make it over the bridge to a flourishing, genuine faith are pretty bleak. But we know it doesn't have to be that way. You can beat the odds. That's why we wrote *Firsthand*. We believe this book can make a big difference to a lot of people—including you—starting today. Our hope is that this book will be an honest source of strength and discussion if you're cynical about the church, new to Christianity, or just trying to strengthen your faith.

In the chapters ahead, we lay out key truths that have helped us in our pursuit of a firsthand faith, and it is our hope and prayer that they will change the way you view your own spiritual journey. We tackle the problem areas and challenges that most young people face when they decide to really experience firsthand faith.

We have heard so many in our generation ask the same agonizing questions that we were asking—questions that we believe must be asked and answered in order to break away from dead religion. Maybe you've asked some of these questions too:

- If God is real, then why do I feel so empty on the inside? (chapter 2)
- Why should I even try to follow God when I feel like such a spiritual failure all the time? (chapter 3)
- I can't stand people who are fakes on the outside, but how do I experience real change that's more than skin deep? (chapter 4)
- Can anyone show me how to enjoy a close relationship with God instead of just checking off a spiritual to-do list every day? (chapter 5)
- How can I develop a strong faith when I'm filled with doubts and questions about God? (chapter 6)
- Can I break free from my comfortable existence and do something *huge* with my life? (chapter 7)
- If I joined a community of others who take first-hand faith seriously, could I really experience lasting change? (chapter 8)

Each chapter is really a description of our journey into seeking answers to those questions and understanding more of who God is and how He wants to relate to us. We have tried to turn theology into authentic experience.

And then we want to share with you some practical ideas

that are helping us grow closer to Christ in ways that are honest and relevant to our generation. At the end of each chapter, you will find a section called "Making It Real," which has three parts:

- "Other Voices"—compelling quotes and stories from people we interviewed for this book
- "Think About It"—reflection questions to help you process and apply what you read in the chapter
- "Might Try This"—a menu of action steps you can take, alone or in a group, to live out what you've learned

All of this is deeply rooted in our own spiritual journeys. We've discovered that before we can get where we want to go, we have to start where we are.

Deconstruction

We've noticed that personal faith always starts on the inside. And at least for us, that meant taking a step back to examine our faith and really decide what belonged and what didn't. It meant going back to the start of our relationship with Christ. We had to go back to the simplicity of a relationship with Christ and brick by brick start building something new and fresh with Him. It was as if God had to deconstruct the nice and tidy religion we had pieced together over the years so we could start from scratch to find what was real.

We began this deconstruction by examining the life of Christ. From attending Sunday school, we knew every Bible story about Jesus, but for the first time we began digging into the Bible and studying the books of the New Testament for ourselves. We no longer bought the "because the Bible tells me so" answers. So we studied other historical texts, watched as many documentaries as we could get our hands on, and tried to expose ourselves to as many different viewpoints as possible. After reading countless books written by atheists, agnostics, Christians, Jews, and people with other beliefs, we were able to rediscover the foundation of our faith.

God had to deconstruct the nice and tidy religion we had pieced together over the years so we could start from scratch to find what was real.

We were primarily dissecting the life of Christ and looking for reasons either to doubt or accept what the Gospels say about who He is and what He did for us. One of the best resources in our research was the book *More Than a Carpenter* by Josh McDowell. (We recommend it to you if you're where we were at this stage.) After looking at all the evidence, we decided for ourselves that Jesus Christ was who He claimed to be.

Today we believe more boldly than ever that Jesus was the

Son of God. That He lived a perfect life. That He died for the entire world's sin and was resurrected three days later and ascended to heaven. That only through faith in Him can we be rescued from our brokenness and find new, everlasting life.

But if you don't agree with this view of Jesus or aren't sure what you believe about Him, we want you to do what we did.

Question what we just said about Jesus.

Seriously.

Clear your thoughts of all your preconceived notions. Look past shallow, judgmental Christians and superficial religion. Look past your bad experiences with church. Start with the life of Christ. Dig into what He said and did. Tell God you want to find the truth, and ask Him to help you find your way through your doubts and confusion.

He's eager to do it. And the experience will turn your life upside down, changing your future forever.

As Paul put it, "It is by your own faith that you stand firm" (2 Corinthians 1:24, NLT).

We have no problem encouraging you to question the Lord. Why? Because He invites us to do that. "Taste and see that the LORD is good," He says (Psalm 34:8). Also, we truly believe in a God who is active and alive in our lives. So if there is any truth to what we believe, a loving God will reveal Himself to those who search for answers.

Saying No to Secondhand Religion

Turning your life over to God and asking Jesus Christ to save you from your sins is the most important step toward firsthand living. That's where your spiritual journey with God starts.

Unfortunately, for so many young people who grew up in church, that's about as far as they go. They get saved, then they sort of sleepwalk through everything else.

That's kind of what we did. We experienced firsthand faith when we placed our faith in the hands of Jesus Christ. But then, as the years went by, we kept falling back into a religion of second-hand knowledge rather than firsthand relationship.

A lot of people we talked to attested to the same kind of problem.

A guy from Georgia named Joey, looking back on his teen-age years, told us, "I had a strong case of what I call 'piggyback religion,' meaning I had confused being in a close relationship with my parents, who had a close relationship with God, with actually being close to God myself."

Heather from Huntsville, Alabama, went through the same thing. "Because you respect your parents, Sunday school teachers, and preachers, you believe what they say," she explained. "They study the Bible and know it, so therefore they must know what they're talking about. It makes it too easy to say, 'I believe because it's what I learned at church.' But what we really need to do is read the Bible and see for ourselves what the pastor is talking about."

The lifestyle of unexamined, secondhand faith doesn't work—and that's what we want to help free you of!

The lifestyle of unexamined, secondhand faith doesn't work.

You won't believe the difference it makes. Right now we're both experiencing an incredible, awe-inspiring, frightening, fulfilling, overwhelming, uncomfortable, and exhilarating journey of firsthand faith. We are still figuring things out and making mistakes along the way, but instead of getting us down, these moments inspire us to grow closer to a God of love and promise.

Most important, we know it's the kind of personally owned faith that no one but God can give you. You can't get it from your parents or friends. You also can't get it from us. But we are going to do everything we can to help you find a firsthand faith that is authentic and unique to you.

So we challenge you to join us on this journey into firsthand Christian faith that matters—and that's all yours. What's so amazing about genuine Christianity (compared to other religions) is that it leads us step by step toward a God who is so much more than an idea or a force. He is a God we can actually know for ourselves, a Person we can have a firsthand relationship with.

Let us tell you what we mean.

Your Name on God's Hands

The most important thing to know about a more personal faith is just how personal God is. We like to put it this way: a firsthand faith starts with realizing what is written on God's hands. Look at what God says in Isaiah 49:15–16: "I will not forget you. I have engraved you on the palms of my hands" (God's Word).

In the original context, God was talking to the people of Judah who were going to come back to Him from their exile in Babylon. But it's also true for all prodigal sons and daughters, anyone who is feeling exiled or separated from Him. Even you.

Just think about it for a moment. The God who created the galaxies and the infinite universe has written your name on the palm of His hands! God knows your name. God knows every detail of your life. He knows the deepest longings of your heart. He knows your darkest secrets, your greatest fears, and your unspoken dreams. And He's crazy about you! He cares deeply about every personal detail of your life.

He didn't just doodle your name on a heavenly scratch pad—He engraved your name on His skin. God has a permanent tattoo of your name on His hands.

The God who has your name tattooed on His hands wants you to experience a firsthand faith so much that He came to this earth and stretched out His hands to willingly take the nails of our selfishness and sin.

Our whole aim in writing this book is to show you that

there's so much more to Christianity than living by someone else's faith. More, too, than being good, going to church, or following the rules. It's about a relationship with the One who fed five thousand hungry people—people just like you and me. It's about quenching your thirst at the Source.

Jesus is the Living Water.

However, if you're looking for six easy steps to happiness, you won't find them in these pages. Life is way more complex than any of us will ever be able to comprehend. So we don't claim to have all the answers. We do, however, invite you to journey with us across the bridge of faith—from a childhood faith to a grown-up, real, firsthand faith.

We spent years living with a faith that was partly our own but mostly someone else's. You don't have to.

Starting now, you can begin to make your life with God a very real, very personal, and absolutely motivating experience. After all, according to the dictionary definition, the word *firsthand* means "direct from the original source."

> You can begin to make your life with God a very real, very personal, and absolutely motivating experience.

That's the kind of life you were created for, the only kind that lasts, and the only kind Jesus came to give.

Making It Real

Other Voices

Read the following quotes from people just like you who have struggled with what it means to follow God, and see how their experiences relate to your own.

I was at church every time the doors opened. I led prayers for my sports teams. I even started a petition so that we could have student-led prayer at my high school graduation. I did that because that was what was expected of the pastor's grandson. The breakthrough for me didn't come until I was twenty-four years old and my mother had a heart attack. I realized then that when she died, my faith would die too if I didn't develop my own faith. —*Anthony from Lexington, Kentucky*

Growing up, I viewed my church as a people who went through the motions but did not live out their faith. Even though this turned me off for a while, it helped me recognize the real thing—authentic and passionate faith—later in life. —*Jeanette from Loudonville, Ohio*

Nothing is "owned" unless you've struggled to own it in some way. A car that is given is a great gift, but the car I worked for is *mine*. It's the same with faith—if it's given to me, I don't value it much. When I've fought through the crap of this world to discover Jesus, it means so much more. —*Luke from Kenosha, Wisconsin*

Firsthand faith is what gets you through the mess. Secondhand faith is what gets you into a lot of messes in the first place. Firsthand faith is solid—you can grab it and hang on to it. Secondhand faith is about as solid as Jell-O. When you really have to hold it tight, it gushes away. —*Jeremiah from Waterford, Michigan*

When you see God moving in your actions, and not your parents' actions, your faith becomes more real. When you recognize truth from discovering what you truly believe instead of just what your grandparents believe, it is like seeing the sky for the first time. It's fun to actually be a part of something rather than just a card-carrying member. —*Ethan from Cardington, Ohio*

Think About It

Use these reflection questions to think about how to apply what you've read in the chapter.

1. On a scale from one to ten, how real and vital would you say your faith is right now? (One means "I'm not sure I even have a personal faith in Christ," while ten means "My faith is really changing me and bringing fulfillment to my life.") Why did you choose that number?

2. Who have been the strongest influences on your faith so far in your life (your parents, friends, youth pastor…)? To what extent is your faith based on what *they* believe, and to what extent is it based on what *you* believe?

3. Have you felt a need to make your faith more your own? Where are you in that process?

4. What kind of faith would you like to have five years from now? How would that faith add meaning and fulfillment to your life?

Might Try This

The ideas that follow are some action steps you might want to take to put the principles of this chapter into practice.

● Join the online firsthand community.

Go to FirsthandBook.com and join the community talking honestly about their "firsthand experiences." You will find practical tools and hear other people's stories as you discover your own firsthand faith.

● Start a firsthand group of your own.

We've found that it's incredibly helpful to discover firsthand faith with friends who share your longing for honesty and encouragement on your journey. So we recommend you read this book and decide on a few trusted friends you'd like in your group and give them a call.

If you want an engaging way to study *Firsthand* with others, we recommend you use the video curriculum we have created. The weekly sessions enhance your firsthand experience by using short films designed to spark discussion. Available in Christian bookstores and at FirsthandBook.com, it's perfect for small groups and youth groups.

● Start a journal.

Going from secondhand faith to a firsthand relationship is a journey. So get yourself a notebook, or use a computer, and start taking notes about where you are on that journey. Include questions, verses, doubts, insights, frustrations, prayers, observations, or whatever else you want to record about what's happening in your life through this transition.

● **Get to know Jesus all over again.**

Read one of the Gospels—Matthew, Mark, Luke, or John—from start to finish. Afterward, write down what you learned about who Jesus is. How does this picture challenge your beliefs and show you areas where you need to change?

2

Soul Thirst
A Faith That Fills the Emptiness

You must be emptied of that of which
you are full, so that you may be filled
with that of which you are empty.

—Augustine

We are half-hearted creatures, fooling
about with drink and sex and ambition
when infinite joy is offered us, like an
ignorant child who wants to go on
making mud pies in a slum because he
cannot imagine what is meant by the
offer of a holiday at sea.

—C. S. Lewis

L ooking back at my life, I (Josh) can still feel it—an inner frustration and emptiness constantly simmering inside.

Ryan and I had grown up in a family where faith was central, and years earlier I had made a personal decision to place my faith in Christ. Toward the end of high school, however, I began living with a nagging sense of defeat when it came to my faith. I tried to block out the emptiness, tried to make myself believe that my life was fine and act like everything was okay. But when I was honest with myself, I had to admit that I wasn't happy. I was overwhelmed with the list of things I was supposed to do— *and* the list of things I definitely wasn't supposed to do. Following the rules had once been satisfying, but at this point the rules made me feel more isolated from God, not closer.

The worst part was that no matter how "good" I was, I never felt content with the choices I made or the person I was. And I felt like there was no one I could talk to about it. If I admitted that I was unhappy and that something was missing from my faith, people might be disappointed in me. God might be disappointed in me.

And I know for a fact that everything I've said describes Ryan's experience too—pretty much word for word.

Do you relate to what we're saying?

When we forget that Christianity is all about a relationship with Christ and we start to settle for the kind of Christianity where we check off our to-do lists for God, then we inevitably experience the emptiness of religion. Religion is all about human-kind trying to work its way into God's approval, and that always leaves an emptiness and ache in the soul.

Empty religion shows up when someone tries to follow rules and rituals to earn salvation, but it also shows up when a Christ follower starts trying to be a "good Christian" so God will love him or her more. What I hadn't realized is that empty religion can sneak into our lives when we forget the purpose of sound spiritual disciplines such as a daily Bible reading and quiet time.

My daily quiet time became something I felt I'd better do so God would approve of me rather than an opportunity to spend time with the God who already approves of me because of Christ's sacrifice. Instead of seeing my daily devotional as a chance to spend time with the God who loves me uncondition-ally, I had turned it into a religious activity that left me feeling defeated. It became one more thing I needed to check off my list to keep God happy, and I failed so often to do all the things on my spiritual checklist that I pretty much gave up.

Most of us can't keep that up for very long.

Somewhere along the way Ryan and I gave up on doing "the

right things" and started trying new things that promised to fill our emptiness. We stopped hanging out with the "church crowd" and started hanging out with whoever seemed to be having the most fun. But after the party was over and the high was gone, we found ourselves right back in that place of emptiness. Only this time the feeling was intensified.

Our souls were thirsty and desperately needed to be quenched. But sometimes things need to get worse before they get better.

THE GIFT OF EMPTINESS

When I (Josh) went off to college, it really hit me that I was alone—without friends, without family, and without anyone else to take responsibility for my faith. It was just God and me, and no one could force me into a relationship with Him. At that point the emptiness of my relationship with my Creator became impossible to ignore. What had been frustration mixed with rebellion now turned to stark desperation.

We are created to desire the Creator, purposefully designed to have longings that only He can fill. George Barna wrote in *Maximum Faith,* "The emptiness or frustration you feel reflects your failure to partner with God to grasp the meaning, purpose, wisdom, character and fulfillment He intends for you to have."[6] In order to receive any gift, you have to draw near to the giver; you have to know the one who has a gift in store for you.

I'll admit it took painful feelings of desperation to push me to draw near to God.

That's when I finally realized that emptiness is not always a bad thing. In fact, it can be a divine gift! It was the pain of my emptiness that drove me to become desperate enough to fall into the arms of the only One who could fill my deepest needs. As I look back, I see that all along it was God Himself who gave me the gift of emptiness.

The way Ryan and I see it, God loves us so much and so greatly desires a deep and real relationship with us that He created us to feel the pain of emptiness until we give up and fall into His ocean of fullness.

God created us to feel the pain of emptiness until we give up and fall into His ocean of fullness.

Without the gift of emptiness, we would never experience how real and fulfilling a relationship with our Creator can be. It's the pain of emptiness that can wake us up and help us break out of religiosity and become desperate for a rich and rewarding relationship with God.

Two things are certain when you turn faith into religion and try to do all the right things to get God's approval. Number one: you feel empty inside. Number two: you always fail! That's because religion isn't the same thing as a real relationship and because there is no way in the world that on our own we could work our way up to God's approval.

This is the point of the Christian faith. God knew there was no chance for us to ever be good enough or to follow enough rules to gain His approval. Since we could never work our way up to God through religion, God came down to us! Christ came to us and went to the cross and took on Himself all our sins and failures and crucified man-made religion so we could experience a full relationship with the heavenly Father.

Now I'm almost grateful for that horrible desperation I felt when I let the faith of my childhood dwindle into nothing more than empty religion. I'm also grateful that I felt even emptier when I turned away from God and looked for fulfillment in foolish and selfish escapes. When we try to anesthetize our pain with partying, drugs, porn, or a million other things, we get only a temporary fix. Then, when it's over, God allows us to feel our real need even more deeply.

Without facing up to what I didn't have, I probably would have never turned to the Source of true filling.

A student named Ashley learned the same lesson I did.

A SECOND CHANCE

When Ashley was living at home in Nashville, Tennessee, she attended a Christian school, went on mission trips, and even gave youth sermons at her church. She believed her faith was solid. So did her parents, who were youth ministers at their home church.

But once Ashley arrived at the University of Georgia for her freshman year, things changed. She was quickly caught up in the social life at college and was striving for excitement and a good time. She began drinking at parties night after night and seeing a string of guys. Cultivating a real relationship with God slipped to the bottom of her priority list.

At first Ashley thought she could handle her new lifestyle, no problem. "I was having so much fun with all the boys and with all the partying, with all the friends," she recalled later. "It didn't really occur to me that I was missing something."

But by her sophomore year, a terrible sense of meaningless-ness set in for Ashley. Was the person she had become really the person she wanted to be?

And how could she be having so much fun and yet be miser-able at the same time? That really took her by surprise.

When she was honest with herself, she knew what she needed to do. She had to go back to Christ and to a life that was centered on Him. So she joined a campus ministry group, began reading the Bible and praying again, and started dating a young man who had been through the same kind of spiritual detour in col-lege and therefore understood her.

Looking back on the experience, Ashley said, "We learn from our struggles and from our temptations and from our mess-ups, and every time we fall, we get back up and we know we are given a second chance."[7]

Ashley's story is way too common among people our age. And one of our greatest hopes for you is that you'll be able to discover a firsthand faith without having to go through the "lost years" of high school or college. Still, for a lot of us, it takes years of mistakes and failed attempts at fulfillment to realize how desperately we need an authentic relationship with Christ.

Breakthrough

It's a pretty strange dynamic when you think about it—first you feel empty, then you get miserable, then you get desperate…and finally you change.

But it's only strange if you're looking at the *what* and ignoring the *why*. By *why,* we mean why would a loving God let us get in such a desperate situation? Could feelings of emptiness and desperation actually be the door to something most of us wouldn't find in any other way?

We think so. In Jesus's most famous sermon, the Sermon on the Mount, He has something to say about this very thing. And it's good news: "You're blessed when you're at the end of your rope. With less of you there is more of God and his rule" (Matthew 5:3, MSG).

You're blessed when you're at the end of your rope? Even

though Jesus's words sound completely backward, He knew something that few of us ever stop to consider: *We can't be filled with God until we're emptied of ourselves!*

That's always the *why* of desperation in God's plan. Before we can find fulfillment, we must feel our own longing. The reason God allows those painful feelings, it seems, is so we'll become desperate for a full relationship with Him.

The reason God allows painful feelings is so we'll become desperate for a full relationship with Him.

And God has to get our attention. For example, He uses fear to wake us up. Your mom and dad are fighting with each other more than ever. You realize that the next big test will determine whether you have to retake the class or get to move on. You find out that your best friend lied to you about something really important, and you're worried about what this will mean for the future of the relationship.

These kinds of anxious things wake us up. They pull us out of the doldrums of a life of safety we have created for ourselves and remind us that we need more of God than we had before.

But if fear is God's wake-up call, then desperation is His fire alarm. Your father passed suddenly from a stroke. The love of your life left you for someone else. You lost your job and have no idea how you'll pay for school. You're at the end of your rope. The hurt seems to overwhelm and outweigh everything good in your life.

In a word, you're desperate.

But what if, at that very moment, you're also one step away from being blessed?

One of the people we surveyed for this book, Linda from Pennsylvania, told us that after she prayed to accept Christ into her life, she didn't feel any different for years. Then suddenly that changed. "After an encounter with God on one of my darkest, most desperate nights," she wrote to us, "I knew that God knew me. I began to realize that even though I wasn't always close to Him, He was close to me."

"One of my darkest, most desperate nights"—she was at the end of her rope. That's where Linda found God and where her faith began to be real. She never would have asked for that dark, desperate night, but it turned out to be just what she needed to transform her relationship with God completely.

She said, "Over time my dependence on God grew, and now there isn't much time that I don't think about Him, talk to Him, thank Him."

Similarly, Karl from West Point, Utah, tells a dramatic story to explain how he woke up to his need for a real relationship with

God. He started out as a classic secondhand-faith kid. As he put it, "I grew up in church and always 'knew' that I was a Christian. I went to Sunday school, sang in the youth choir, went to church camp, went through confirmation. I had one of my first kisses at a youth fellowship meeting. It was my social life, but there was nothing transformational about it."

Years later Karl was in his twenties and serving in the United States Army in South Korea when he was a passenger on a helicopter that crashed due to a mechanical malfunction. He wasn't badly injured, but his spiritual life would never be the same. "That crash symbolized my life in a lot of ways," he said. "As I cried out to God, I realized that He had much more in store for me than just going to church on Sunday and that being a Christian meant more than a social life. It had to be a way of life. No longer was it okay to say a prayer and then, sure of a place in heaven, go forth to sin happily ever after."

Who would have thought that a helicopter crash would be a good thing?

No matter how much it hurts, "at the end of your rope" can be a very good place! You have nothing to lose and a lot to gain. You might finally be ready for less of you and more of God. You might just be at the door of the real, personal faith you've always wanted and desperately needed.

Augustine, a father of the early church whom we cite at the

top of this chapter, referred to the promise of this moment when he wrote, "You must be emptied of that of which you are full, so that you may be filled with that of which you are empty."

Emptied. It's at end-of-the-rope moments like these that we drop flimsy and untested hand-me-down beliefs that don't really fit us anyway. We dump secondhand beliefs and empty religion… and finally reach for something real.

Dying of Soul Thirst

You might know the New Testament story about a woman who was near the end of her rope. We don't know her name— she's just called the Samaritan woman. (Read her story in John 4:4–42.) Jesus meets her at a well in the hottest, dustiest part of the day. She is alone, busily filling her water jars, when Jesus asks if she could spare Him a drink.

She hesitates. Samaritans and Jews weren't supposed to be seen together. "Um…well…" She nervously stalls.

And then Jesus says, "If you knew…who it is that asks you for a drink, you would have asked him and he would have given you living water" (verse 10).

See, Jesus knew she suffered from a deeper need than thirst. In the gentle conversation that follows, she admits as much. Her life isn't going well—she's alone, rejected, on the losing end of a long string of bad relationships.

Desperate, you say? Empty? This woman is *dying* inside because of the life she leads!

When she asks for some of His "living water," Jesus tells her, "Whoever drinks the water I give him will never thirst. Indeed, the water I give him will become in him a spring of water welling up to eternal life" (verse 14). Then Jesus reveals to her something truly amazing—He is the Messiah she has been waiting for.

That one conversation changed her life. The Bible says that the woman rushed back to the village to spread the news about Jesus and that many "believed in him because of the woman's testimony" (verse 39).

It's what you do with your deep, inner craving that makes all the difference.

Of course, every person in the village who heard the woman's story desperately needed the same living water Jesus offered. There wasn't one among them who needed Jesus less. They all lived with a craving for God whether or not they knew it or would admit to it. There were simply those who realized how desperate they were and believed and were filled, and those who didn't and remained empty.

Everyone is truly in a spiritually desperate situation, completely dependent on a close relationship with God. It's just that sometimes, out of pride, we don't see it. That's the main thing we're trying to show you in this chapter. It's what you do with that deep, inner craving that makes all the difference.

WE'RE ALL DESPERATE

Just like the woman at the well, I (Ryan) have felt empty. Craving fulfillment. Desperate for relief deep inside.

But that inner ache helped me finally break through my wall of pride. I admitted my desperation to God and a couple of close friends. I even got up the courage to open up to my parents about my feelings. Instead of judging me or telling me how disappointed they were in me, they did something completely different. I'll never forget it. Mom and Dad began to share with me that they too had felt much the same way at times and could totally relate! The revelation that my parents had felt this way convinced me that desperation, discouragement, and emptiness weren't limited to me and my friends. They are actually essential to experiencing a loving God's unstoppable pursuit of our affections. But we'll get back to that.

Seeing how common my situation was, I put together a short film titled *Empty*, which expressed how I and so many others feel. It struck a chord with people of all ages. For example, a successful sixty-year-old businessman told me that he teared up when he watched it because it described exactly how he felt.

Whether you're a pastor or a prostitute, a teenager or a teacher, a businessman or a homeless man, you should know that we've all received the divine gift of emptiness. The question is, are you desperate enough to let it lead you to a satisfaction that lasts—a deeply satisfying firsthand faith?

A FIRSTHAND LIFE

When I (Ryan) was thirteen, our family took a two-day summer road trip from our home in Houston to Big Bend National Park in West Texas. Days before we left I planned what I would do on the car ride. I managed to bring just about all my earthly possessions, including my Game Boy, a shelf's worth of books, magazines, my Xbox, a portable TV, and an assortment of beverages (which I refused to share with my siblings). I was giddy with excitement about how amazing this car ride was going to be. I had so much to do, so much to keep me entertained. No way would I be bored on this trip!

About an hour into the trip I had given up on the video game I was playing, put down the book I never opened, and had to go to the bathroom. My amazing car trip now consisted of staring out the window while my sister played her pop music. All my awesome activities and entertainment somehow lost their appeal after sitting still in the backseat of our crowded Suburban. The whole experience was made worse by the fact that all my earthly possessions surrounding me limited my mobility to looking out the window.

This was not the amazing trip I had planned.

When we finally arrived at Big Bend—and I had wiped all

the fast-food crumbs off my pants—I looked up in awe. My mouth hung open for about a minute while I twirled around in a 360. I had never seen a sky so blue or mountain ranges so amazing. I took a deep breath of fresh, crisp mountain air. Even though the air was thinner than I was used to, it was as if I was breathing oxygen for the first time.

I said to myself, *God is so much bigger than I can understand.*

That vacation at Big Bend was one of the most fun weeks of my life. Our family went horseback riding and hiking and enjoyed each other's company. Every moment at the national park felt exciting and new. I was totally alive in the moment and was enjoying each activity with my entire being. I didn't hold back my laughter or excitement. I lived my days to the fullest during that week in Big Bend. I had heard from other people how beautiful the national parks were, but now I was experiencing the beauty of God's creation firsthand.

On the road trip of life, are you feeling unfulfilled by your own plans and desires? Do you feel confined to looking out the window, just imagining what might be better? Like me on that car ride, maybe you've been piling junk into your life, hoping it will make you happy, only to realize that you are more empty than ever before.

The incredible truth Josh and I want to share is that God desires for every day of your life to feel like that week I had at Big Bend. He wants you to live life to the fullest, with no hesitation and no regrets and with overflowing joy. He's waiting for you to abandon all the unhealthy habits, relationships, and junk that you're grasping at to find fulfillment. This book is meant to act as a guide as you learn to let go of your plans and step into God's purpose for your life.

> God is waiting for you to abandon all the unhealthy habits, relationships, and junk that you're grasping at to find fulfillment.

That doesn't mean the journey of life will always be easy. I wish we could say that once you get desperate enough to take your emptiness to God, you will never feel empty again. You and I are still human. We will make mistakes, and our tanks won't always be full. But maybe that's the beauty of it. Every time we start to feel empty, it reminds us to keep coming back to our primal relationship with Christ.

Emptiness and desperation are the greatest reminders that our faith is not simply an aspect of our lives or a cultural inheritance. They point to a God who wants us to experience Him every moment of every day. They are a constant reminder that we were made for (and promised) a greater world free of pain and emptiness.

Maybe that's what being filled with new life is all about. We come to realize that we can depend on Him for everything—no matter what we feel or what comes next—and He will be enough.

Making It Real

Other Voices

After my first year of college, I had a discussion with a peer in which I said that while I knew what I believed was true, I just didn't care about it anymore. God used that year to really hit me hard and make me realize how much I need Him—not just church, but Jesus Himself. —*Luke from Kenosha, Wisconsin*

I hit a "perfect storm" about six or seven years ago. For personal reasons I had to quit college. At the same time I had changed parts in the choir and was majorly struggling. And the young adults' Bible study I'd been trying so hard to get off the ground was going nowhere. The combination led to major depression, and I felt like I'd failed God. I didn't get out of bed for about six months. And it was another four years before I started attending church regularly again. Now, back in church, I am doing something so completely different. It feels like God had an important purpose for all those hard times. —*Debra from Topeka, Kansas*

When I was a junior at a Christian college, I came to a crossroads as I contemplated my future: Would I trust God for my future, or would I continue controlling my life as I'd always done? It was at that point I realized I didn't trust God—I was afraid that if I turned things over to Him, He wouldn't give me what I wanted.

That realization led to some deep soul searching, and I realized that either I needed to claim my faith as my own (rather than coasting on the faith of my parents) or I needed to walk away. I came to the conclusion that what I had been taught about Jesus and His sacrifice was true, and I surrendered my life to Him. —*Becky from Central City, Nebraska*

I just about threw away my marriage. We had been married about a year, but I lived a double life, eventually being unfaithful to my husband.

We separated for two months, and during that time I came to the bottom…and finally hit my knees. It is only by God's grace that our marriage was restored and that I now have a different kind of faith—one that is about more than just doing the right thing. It's about a love that is greater than anything we can ever experience on this earth—a love relationship with our Creator God. —*Paula from Clemmons, North Carolina*

As a seminary student, I was devoting my entire life to vocational ministry and specifically teaching and preaching the gospel. But there were no roots. I was doing it because everyone told me I would make a great pastor or youth minister.

I learned that God was not interested in what I contributed to His kingdom. His interest was in me as a person and in my being conformed to Christ's image. God didn't need me to work; He desired me to know Him intimately. This new perspective not only transformed my heart and mind but redirected my study and ministry. —*Stan from Forney, Texas*

Think About It

1. Would you say that you have drifted away from your old secondhand faith and have been experimenting with living away from God and His commands? If so, what have you been doing or thinking differently?

2. Have you begun to feel spiritual emptiness inside? Do you have friends who have felt the same way?

3. Have you ever felt that you were at the end of your rope— desperate—because your sense of emptiness was so great? Do you have someone in your life you can share your feelings with?

4. How might God want to use your desperation to draw you into a truer, richer relationship with Him?

Might Try This

● Watch the film *Empty*.

Go to FirsthandBook.com/Empty, and watch Ryan's short film *Empty*. Ryan made *Empty* to remind himself and his friends that there is more to the Christian life than what they had settled for. Watch it or share it with a small group of friends so you can discuss the video and voice your opinions. Can you relate to the film? Are you running on empty right now?

● If needed, get help.

If you're not dealing with just the usual young adult's questions about beliefs but are dealing with spiritual abuse, severe depression, or other dangerous circumstances, look for help right away. There are several good organizations, and your local church may be one of the best places to go for help. Seek out a counselor or youth pastor for assistance without judgment.

● Find a mentor.

One thing that can help the most when you are struggling in your faith is to have an older, more mature Christian you can process it all with. If you don't already have such a mentor, ask around and see if you can find one. Again, a pastor at your local church may be a great person to talk to about finding a mentor.

● Keep seeking God.

Even if God seems far away (or you're not even sure He's there), don't give up the spiritual practices of trying to connect with Him—praying, reading the Bible, worshiping. God rewards discipline and patience. So don't give up!

● Consider Jesus's upside-down definitions of happiness.

Slowly, line by line, read Matthew 5:1–12 in The Message, and think about how these Beatitudes blow away your preconceived notions of what real fulfillment is.

● Pray.

Do something a little crazy: ask God to make you as desperate as you have to be to finally turn away from any secondhand faith you may be relying on. Then ask Him to make your life over entirely in the way He wants it to be. What things are you holding on to that God would need to take out of your life so you would come to totally rely on Him?

3

Sick of Secrets

A Faith That Frees

I have come to believe that by and
large the human family all has the
same secrets, which are both very
telling and very important to tell.
They are telling in the sense that
they tell what is perhaps the central
paradox of our condition—that what
we hunger for perhaps more than
anything else is to be known in our
full humanness, and yet that is often
just what we also fear more than
anything else.

—Frederick Buechner

Imagine what it would be like to come alive and experience the freedom of firsthand faith. This might surprise you, but we think that one of the most important payoffs of firsthand faith might be just that—coming alive in emotional and spiritual freedom.

And that's what we were created for. It's in our DNA to crave it. It's the reason Jesus came to earth. We all crave the freedom to be fully ourselves at every moment without holding anything back. And when it comes to our lives as Christians, we all long for a natural, honest, life-giving relationship with God too.

What we long for, however, is usually very different from what we have. But here's the thing: often we're a big part of the problem. Have you noticed how we throw about as much energy into trying to *push away* what we want as trying to *make it real* in our lives? Frederick Buechner wrote, "What we hunger for perhaps more than anything else is to be known in our full humanness, and yet that is often just what we also fear more than anything else."[8]

So what we hunger for is also what we fear? Maybe that's

why we long for freedom but what we experience is more like enslavement.

Can you relate?

Sometimes it's the chains of addiction that enslave us in a constant pursuit of pleasure that never satisfies. Sometimes it's always trying to please our friends that imprisons us in a life of insecurity and fear. Sometimes it's the trap of trying to be "the good Christian kid" who checks off that religious to-do list every day. Whatever it is, we try to keep it to ourselves so that nobody else will know.

Kara from Denver admitted to us, "I have always struggled with being honest with myself, God, and others. Letting people see my failures or the places I struggle in sounds like torture. I have no problem telling them about certain struggles, but you want me to show you my heart in its entirety? Every filthy thing? Yeah, then I don't like that at all."

Nothing unusual there.

Kara's got secrets. We all have secrets.

In this chapter we want to talk about what happens to us when we hold those secrets in. We're going to focus on the enslavement that occurs when we can't seem to measure up to what we know God wants—can't measure up over and over and over again, actually.

In our experience that kind of enslavement leads to living a lie. Covering up. Faking it. You walk around with a secret, pretending you're one thing while inside you know the truth, and the truth sucks, and you feel like a fraud.

And there's nothing firsthand—direct from the original source—about that kind of faith!

As we know from personal experience, living as a slave to a lie will set you up for an endless cycle of shame and guilt. When you feel worthless and ashamed most of the time, getting close to God—or even wanting to—is hard. Really hard. It's easier just to go through the motions. Settle for secondhand religion. Maybe move away from God and church altogether.

Living as a slave to a lie will set you up for an endless cycle of shame and guilt.

Unfortunately, it happens all the time.

But it doesn't have to. Think about what amazing things you could do if you could break free from those feelings of worthlessness and shame. Imagine feeling like you could get close to God without fear of condemnation. Imagine what it would feel like to break free from the cycle of secrets—of beating yourself up with all that shame and guilt.

Your spirit would come alive. Your life would change. You would walk into a world filled with new possibilities.

And you would be free.

Doesn't that sound like what you've always wanted?

FALSE FREEDOM

I (Josh) used to think freedom was to buy what I wanted, go where I wanted, drink what I wanted, watch what I wanted. My definition of freedom was basically doing whatever I wanted, whenever I wanted. What I discovered, however, is that you and I are free to do whatever we choose to do, but once we make that choice, we aren't free anymore. Once we make a choice, we then become bound by the consequences of that choice. For example, you're free to jump off a building, but once you do, you're not free anymore. You are bound by the law of gravity.

When we choose disobedience and sin, we chain ourselves to consequences. Part of the most devastating consequences are the overwhelming feelings of shame and guilt.

I'm all too familiar with shame—where it starts and ends and what it can do to a person. I reached a point during my teenage years when I felt like I couldn't talk to anyone about my sin. Talking to my parents about anything sinful felt awkward, and I was too ashamed to bring my struggle to God. So I kept my sin to myself. I lied, not admitting it to my friends. I never mentioned porn to my dad, and I never prayed to God about my lust.

Eventually my guilt and shame began to crush me. I felt like I was going through life with a one-hundred-pound bag of bricks on my back and a constant knot in my stomach. My shame kept me from connecting with God and others. It paralyzed me to such a degree that I doubted I could ever share the truth about myself with anyone.

But that was a lie. My problem was actually pretty simple. I was sick. Sick from running from the truth, from trying to make everyone believe a lie. Sick from having no one I could talk to. Sick of myself too. Sick deep down in my soul.

> I was sick. Sick from running from the truth. Sick deep down in my soul.

Does that sound like you? Sick and growing sicker every day from an ailment you can't name? Do you feel like you're carrying a hundred pounds of bricks on your shoulders? If so, you should know it doesn't have to be that way. You can live differently, starting now.

REAL FREEDOM

One of the most liberating and powerful statements of all time comes from the lips of Jesus: "You will know the truth, and the truth will set you free" (John 8:32). And we're writing this chapter to tell you something that will set you free. The only way we've been able to experience freedom is by *making the choice to get completely gut-level honest with God and others.*

Here's how I (Josh) did it.

I finally went to God and just unloaded the ugly truth about my secret sins. All of it. I said the words out loud to Him, even though He already knew every "secret" I had to tell.

And then I did something else. I took the risk of sharing my secret struggles with my friend Dave. We have been friends since junior high, and although both of us have struggled with our faith and made countless stupid, immature decisions, we've always shared a desire to be godly men. I figured if I could be honest with anyone, it would be Dave.

Once we started talking, it didn't take long for me to discover that he was just as frustrated as I was at how easy it is to be fake about our faith, to compartmentalize things about ourselves we're ashamed of, and to act like we have everything together. He was sick and tired of secrets too.

We decided to talk with each other once a week and be 100 percent honest about our lives, our faith, and our struggles. We wanted to be completely vulnerable. As painful as it was at first to talk about my failures and sins and ask for prayer, good things started to happen right away. I didn't feel so alone. I felt new freedom to be myself. And my relationship with the Lord began to change in a radical way. I felt free to come to Him with my sins and struggles and accept His forgiveness and grace. I had stumbled into what this book is about—a real, raw, firsthand relationship with the One who made us.

I am discovering that when we refuse to get real with others, it is unloving to them. When we hide who we are from the people closest to us, it just downplays our relationship with them. When I try to stay at the surface level with my friends instead of going deeper and trying to find out what is really going on in their lives, I am essentially telling them, "I don't love you enough to risk awkwardness and get real with you."

If we truly believe that the death of Jesus Christ sets us free from all guilt and sin, and if that forgiveness comes from Him alone, what good does it do to live as if we still carry these burdens? We can be totally honest and open about our brokenness because our mistakes and shortcomings no longer matter. At all! Our security and identity are found, not in our ability to hide our shame or overcome our addictions and desires, but in God's perfection and unconditional mercy. That should be something we cannot help but get excited about!

Our security and identity are found, not in our ability to hide our shame, but in God's unconditional mercy.

I once heard someone say that we're only as sick as our secrets, and I couldn't agree more. When I finally revealed my struggles and sins to God and my friend, I started to heal on the inside. You will too.

And I'm still making a deliberate effort to be open with my friend. Yes, Dave and I have to constantly work at it, and some weeks (or months!) are better than others. But we don't give up on each other. It is so important to be real with the people you care about.

Telling the truth, even if it isn't pretty, is like oxygen for a long-distance runner. It fills you with strength. And it's not optional. If you want an authentic, living, firsthand faith, it's where you start.

We all know people who put Bible verses or prayers on their Facebook statuses or tweets. I am not saying that is wrong or that they are being dishonest or anything like that. On the contrary, it can be very encouraging. But when do you ever see a tweet that says, "Where are You, God? I need You. Why have You left me?" When did you see a tweet that said, "I feel like a total failure, and it's killing me" or "Why can't I tell you who I really am?"

We are so ready to let the world know when God is doing great things. Yet when things take a turn for the worse, we keep it hidden. What are we so afraid of?

There has rarely been a time in my life when I have been able to say, "God, things absolutely suck right now, but I know You are in control." Honestly, most of the time my prayer is, "God, things absolutely suck right now. Where were You when that happened?"

As time goes on, I hope I get better at recognizing the Lord's faithfulness. I want my relationship with God to be real. I am tired of going through the motions, and I am convinced it is better to be honest than to say the "right" thing. God knows how we are really feeling, anyway, and He knows how little we understand about the way He works.

Our Weakness, His Power

Every important figure or leader in Scripture had obvious weaknesses that the Lord used to reveal Himself to others. After he committed adultery, King David wrote a prayer that millions have prayed over the centuries. Maybe you're familiar with it. Part of it says:

> Create in me a pure heart, O God,
>   and renew a steadfast spirit within me. (Psalm 51:10)

And then there's the apostle Paul, leader of the early church. He wrote honestly about his struggle with sin when he said, "I do not understand what I do. For what I want to do I do not do, but what I hate I do" (Romans 7:15). He even called himself the worst of sinners, stating that if God can save him, He can save anybody (1 Timothy 1:15–16).

So why should we spend all this effort trying to pose as something we're not?

God can use you and me through our brokenness, but first we have to get real and vulnerable with Him and with others. I think this powerful "get real" dynamic works for a few reasons.

First of all, being real with God and those around us invites us to drop the pride and pretense and to walk in humility.

Second, honesty invites us to live every day in gratitude for the incredible grace the Lord has shown us.

And third, since now we know we can't make it on our own—and that's okay—we're ready to invite God's power to do for us what we can't do for ourselves. Paul said in 2 Corinthians 12:9, "I will boast all the more gladly about my weaknesses, so that Christ's power may rest on me."

This turns our concept of weakness and vulnerability on its head. We are not saying that God *makes up* for our weaknesses. We are admitting that He is ready to work *through* them. Our weaknesses can actually become our greatest assets because they draw us closer to the Lord. And once we see how God can use them, we have all the more reason to be open about our struggles.

> Our weaknesses can become our greatest assets because they draw us closer to the Lord.

For example, a huge struggle for most guys we've talked to is pornography. Even though I am not as honest about it as I should be all the time, I do my best to talk to my friends, my dad, and my brothers about it. Bringing sin out into the light in this way forces me to confront it, and the only way I could do that is by going to the Lord. It is not like the problem goes away. My battle with lust will never just be over and done with. I go to my friends because I know they won't judge me and so they can share similar struggles with me. And I go to the Lord because I know He will accept me as I am. He will help me live with integrity. He is ready to save me from myself—and I know how desperately I need a Savior and always will.

Worship at a Time of Weakness

Realizing how much we need both God's grace and His power might sound to you like lofty theology. But it's not. It's down-to-earth, practical stuff. Once we truly begin to think of weakness as a gift, we can quit pretending we're something we're not. We can stop holding on to the secrets that are killing us. We can drop the wimpy secondhand faith and worn-out religious rules that aren't working anyway.

We can finally get real with God.

And—here's the best part—God can finally become more real to us.

I (Josh) was talking with Dave one night after he was having a particularly tough week. "I just feel like Job," he said. "I feel like I'm doing all the right things and not one single thing is going right in my life."

Dave was being real. At the time I didn't know quite what to say, so I mostly listened and did my best to show my friend that

I care. But what Dave said got me thinking, and when I got home, I read through some of Job. Maybe you know his story. He was a man who had everything, and in rapid succession God allowed all of it to be taken away—his family, his wealth, his health—because Satan wanted to see whether Job would curse the Lord if he lost everything he had been blessed with.

> Once we begin to think of weakness as a gift, we can get real with God. And God can become more real to us.

Job's response went against everything I grew up learning, even as a Christian. After everything that happened, Job tore his clothes and began to…worship. He said:

Naked I came from my mother's womb,
   and naked I will depart.
The LORD gave and the LORD has taken away;
   may the name of the LORD be praised. (Job 1:21)

As crazy as this response sounds, should it really be surprising? Job was not superspiritual or perfect. Not at all. Bottom line: he recognized that he deserved absolutely nothing. He knew he was sinful. Imperfect. Broken. Faulty. Weak. Every good thing he enjoyed had come from the Lord. He didn't deserve any of it.

If the Lord took it away, so be it. Experiencing it for a short time was a greater blessing than he deserved. Notice that Job wasn't dancing and clapping his hands in his worship as he spoke. He didn't try to put on a mask of fake happiness when his soul was in torment. But he responded with an earnest and joyful heart even though his life had been broken. Job cried out to his Father with a heart of praise.

The beautiful thing is that Job's response to his own faults and weaknesses was what made him so remarkable in the eyes of the Lord. And it made room for his faith to grow. Being authentic with himself and with God allowed Job to trust in the Lord in even the worst circumstances.

Of course, getting honest doesn't mean everything will turn out perfectly. But it does restore a right relationship between a worship-worthy God and one of His worship-ready children.

Forgiven and Free

Earlier we shared a verse with you from John 8, but now we want to show you more of that chapter to give you a broader context. In John 8:34–36, Jesus said, "I tell you most solemnly that anyone who chooses a life of sin is trapped in a dead-end life and is, in fact, a slave. A slave is a transient, who can't come and go at will. The Son, though, has an established position, the run of the house. So if the Son sets you free, you are free through and through" (MSG).

Jesus was saying, "I have truly set you free. You are no longer enslaved to your sin, because of what I have done. I have mastered death, and My mercy and love are so great that you are no longer guilty." That might seem unjust to some. And we are not saying that there are no longer repercussions for our actions. What we *are* saying is that our favor with the Lord, our ability to communicate with the Lord on this earth, and His promise of eternal life free of suffering are secured once we accept His free gift of grace. And that is fantastic news for people like us.

We are completely set free, but what we choose to do with that freedom is what sets apart an authentic, firsthand faith from lifeless religion.

Acceptance is freeing. Love is liberating. God's unconditional love is what encourages and empowers us to live the life of risk and adventure that we have always desired. God's unconditional love is what allows us to risk being honest with Him and others about ourselves.

God's love will never fail us. We will never wear His patience thin or cause Him to stop caring for us. He knows us better than we know ourselves and provides for our needs accordingly. He is the incarnation of love, and His grace and mercy are beyond comprehension. Yet, at the same time, He is absolutely just and all-powerful. Only when we have accepted His grace and entered into a relationship with our Creator are we truly set free. No longer must we fear the possibility of failure, because God will never fail us. No longer do we have to struggle to hide our failings in order to find acceptance, because our God knows our every failing and loves us unconditionally all the time.

So many Christians are able to speak grace and encouragement into others' lives but all the while hate themselves because they know how messed up they are. Many of us resort to self-destructive behavior in light of our faults. We know our sins deserve punishment, and we think we're the best ones to dish it out. People our age have resorted to all kinds of unhealthy self-punishment, trying to right the wrongs inside.

Like Ryan's friend Morgan, who began to cut herself in college because "nothing else had worked." Or like my friend Sam. He had become a Christian but resented himself because he "knew he was doing it all wrong." Hating himself for his sin, he would lock himself in his room for days and often experienced such deep depression that he contemplated suicide.

And sometimes our emotional bondage remains long after the spiritual chains have been broken. That's what happened to me. There were so many times when I asked Christ to forgive me, but I couldn't forgive myself. I kept beating myself up for my past mistakes and sins. I knew in my head that I was forgiven by God, but in my heart I still doubted His grace. I mean, if God really knew all my deepest, darkest secrets, then there was no way He could forgive me for all the sinful mistakes I had made, right?

Sometimes our emotional bondage remains long after the spiritual chains have been broken.

I had felt this way for several years and had all but given up the idea of living without the burden of shame. Then God finally opened my eyes when I felt Him impress this on my heart: *The blood of My Son covers your shame. Who are you not to forgive yourself when I have forgiven you? Do you think you're greater than I am?*

I started to realize then that I'm forgiven whether I feel like it or not. When I share the truth with my Lord, He forgives me, not because I deserve it, but because of who He is. He is the Savior and the Healer, and His grace is unconditional. He knows my most horrible sins, but He chooses to forgive me through the blood of His Son, Jesus Christ.

No Matter What

Lately we've started to have the audacity to believe a simple truth we learned in Sunday school years ago:

Jesus loves me! This I know,
For the Bible tells me so.

Little ones to Him belong;

They are weak, but He is strong.

Could it be that the deepest, most profound truth you will ever learn is found in the first song that most of us learn at church?

Jesus loves me!

When I feel weak and worthless, Jesus loves me!

When I screw up and sin, Jesus loves me!

When I feel like a failure, Jesus loves me!

When I fail a test, Jesus loves me!

When I lose my temper, Jesus loves me!

When I don't feel like loving Him or when I doubt He even exists, Jesus loves me!

When I am unlovable, Jesus loves me!

You may have secrets. In a dark room deep inside, you may be trying to hide sins and failures from yourself, from others, even from God. But now you can let go of the guilt and the shame and move out into the open space of freedom that Jesus created for His people.

God loves you no matter what!

Making It Real

Other Voices

I was cleaning my house for some guests, and everything looked spotless—swept, mopped, vacuumed, and scrubbed clean. But if you had opened just one closet door, you would have been horrified by all the things I stashed in there! That reminded me so much of what my life was like—a hidden mess. I started to confess those sins to God and to others.

The truth is that the closet sins may keep you looking good on the outside, but the dishonesty of them, the need to hide them, and the shame they carry also keep you from knowing God and others in any real and vulnerable way. —*Heather from Gloucester, Virginia*

When I was in college, I used to have trouble getting honest about stuff. There were a few things I did in college that I didn't want people to know about because I said I was a Christian and did them anyway. It wasn't until we had a speaker at chapel who addressed the very things I was struggling with that I was able to get real. Knowing that I wasn't the only one going through it, despite being a Christian, made me feel more comfortable about getting real with others. —*Phronsie from Billings, Montana*

I'm an extremely open and real person, sometimes too real. I'm still working on finding that filter for my mouth! However, I have a couple of things in my life that don't fit at all with who I think I am.

I lived in shame and guilt for quite a while until I realized that God is not a God of guilt and shame; He's a God of light. When I began to bring my struggles to trusted friends and mentors, the hold that guilt and shame had on my life was released. It was very freeing. —*Melissa from Cedar Rapids, Iowa*

I was a member of a small group at my church, and one night the group leader asked me how I was doing. I lost it emotionally. My marriage was failing, and I sobbed in front of the other group members as I let them in on my secret. It was hard to be so transparent with them, yet it felt so good. Once you have that breakthrough and are honest with others about the real you, it gets easier and easier, because you see that they accept you for who you are—failures, flaws, and all. —*Jessica from Burlington, Vermont*

Getting honest with myself about what I need to change in my life to make my walk more Christlike is hard. I'm sure I don't face it as often as I should, but doing it has made me realize the depth of love that Jesus has for me. When I can take that sin or issue to Him and realize that He forgives me and is helping me make the change, that is a beautiful—albeit sometimes painful—experience. Sharing that testimony with others, even if it's only a few, has helped strengthen their walk and given them the freedom to open up and admit their own weaknesses.
—*April from Independence, Missouri*

Think About It

1. What sins or secrets are you trying to hide? How does keeping these secrets make you feel? What is it doing to your life?

2. Whom could you go to when you're ready to start opening up about your secrets?

3. Whom do you need to seek forgiveness from? God? Somebody you let down? Yourself?

4. As you think about Jesus and what He has done, what gives you confidence that you can live free from enslavement to your guilt feelings?

5. If you were to confess your sins and move beyond them, accepting God's forgiveness and releasing the shame, how might that change your life?

Might Try This

● **Share your secret.**

Visit FirsthandBook.com/Secret to read about the secret guilt and shame of others, and see if you can relate to some of them. If you want, you can anonymously share your spiritual secret with us, and we may post it on the Web page for others to read.

● **Journal it.**

You might want to write out your feelings about secrets and shame by following these four steps:

Step 1. My struggles. Write about the secret struggles you've been holding in. We all have them, and we all have a God who loves us, no matter what. The mere act of writing about them can be liberating.

Step 2. My realizations. Then write about how God might be trying to free you to be real and to experience His grace and forgiveness. Even if you're just beginning to get honest, what and who has been most helpful to you in moving toward living in the truth?

Step 3. Payoff for me. Now think about how this process of getting real might be helping you experience a more authentic and meaningful faith. Write down what comes to mind. Then write down what you would like your firsthand faith to look like in five years.

Step 4. Payoff for others. Several people we surveyed talked about how coming clean about their failings helped others do the same. We have found that to be true as well. Write down how your changes in this area are affecting the way you relate to others. How could your honesty allow you to connect better with your friends and family? What would those important relationships look like if they were deeper than surface level?

Study a psalm.

Read Psalm 32, a song lyric that King David wrote to celebrate how great he felt when he stopped holding his sins in and opened up about them to God. Think about which lines reflect how you're feeling. Does the psalm inspire you to pray? to create your own artistic expression of what you're going through? Spend some time with God, and be totally honest with Him about what you've been holding in. Keep at it until you feel unburdened.

Talk to a friend.

I (Josh) had a friend, Dave, whom I could open up with. Whom could you talk to about your struggles? (Be sure to pick somebody you can trust!)

4

Real Faith, Real Change
A Faith That Radically Transforms

I hate all your show and pretense,
The hypocrisy of your praise.

—Jon Foreman

Love from the center of who you are;
don't fake it.

—Romans 12:9 (MSG)

Many Christians act as though once you commit your life to Christ, your whole life comes together and it's "happily ever after."

Sorry. It's just not that way.

I (Ryan) was at a Christian homeless shelter and restoration center in downtown Los Angeles recently, and a man named James shared his story of how Christ was changing his life.

From his worn tennis shoes and plain T-shirt to his weathered face and weary smile, you could tell by looking at James that he had been through a lot. He said that he had been living on the streets and addicted to drugs when he first came to the homeless center. He was caught in a seemingly endless cycle of cocaine and alcohol abuse. He then received Christ into his life and went through the recovery program and began to counsel others. He thought that he had overcome his addiction for good. After a couple of years, however, he returned to the streets and was back on drugs. He lost everything all over again and was right where he had started just a few years earlier.

"I screwed up big time," James told us. "I was living in sin, and I knew it. But you know, the whole time the Lord Jesus never left me."

Your failings and mine might not be quite so obvious as this man's were. But isn't that the way it goes for all of us? Josh and I have already discovered that real life change is messy. It's often three steps forward and two steps back. It's not a neat and tidy "happily ever after" until we get to heaven.

I think the reason so many Christians never reach out to those far from God is that their neat and tidy churches would get too messy. There would be too many tattoos and not enough ties in the church. There would be too many people addicted to drugs and alcohol, too many who have been divorced more than once, too many who have had abortions, too many who have ended up on the wrong side of the law. On and on I could go.

Well, nearly every church actually does have people with all the issues I just described. Every church is filled with broken, messed-up people, by default. It's just that many Christians like to project the image that everything is neat, tidy, and under control. Doesn't it seem that way to you?

In reality, we're all messes. That's why we need more than a makeover—we need real, personal transformation that gets beneath the surface.

But what does real change look like? Where does it come from? And how does it relate to finding and keeping a lifelong, firsthand faith?

That's what this chapter is about.

Firsthand Change

Real change starts when we stop worrying about how spiritual we appear on the outside and start surrendering our messy lives to the God who wants to change us from the inside. We are called to be different from the crowd. Different from the surface-level "perfection" we spend so much effort trying to achieve.

Real change starts when we stop worrying about how spiritual we appear on the outside and start surrendering our messy lives to the God who wants to change us from the inside.

It would mean putting aside all the surface issues—at least long enough to get a grip on what is "good, pleasing and perfect" for us in God's plan. In Romans 12:2, Paul shared what that looks like and how we can experience the deep-down transformation that can make that happen: "Do not conform any longer to the pattern of this world, but be transformed by the renewing of your mind. Then you will be able to test and approve what God's will is—his good, pleasing and perfect will."

The Greek word for *transformed* in this verse literally means "changed from the inside out." If we are serious about making a journey to firsthand fulfillment and transformation, we have to be changed from the inside out. The kind of change that Paul talked about can't occur from external forces. We have to make a conscious decision to embark on this journey. Then we are on the unpredictable and messy path to real change.

When people hear that Christ has called them to radical inner transformation and nonconformity with the world, they often think one of two things. First, some think that being set apart by Christ means they have a free pass to ignore people they don't like or don't want to be associated with. We've seen way too many cliques in youth groups and schools because people felt they were "set apart" or better than others. Being set apart may make us different, but it definitely doesn't make us inherently better than anyone else.

Jesus was always much more concerned with heart issues than surface appearances. The Pharisees of the Bible once asked Jesus why He chose to hang around people who on the surface appeared to be outcasts and sinners. He told them, "It is not the healthy who need a doctor, but the sick. I have not come to call the righteous, but sinners" (Mark 2:17). If our idea of being a Christian is being better than everyone else, then we aren't ready for radical transformation, and any change we undergo will probably be no more than skin deep.

The second reaction some people have when they hear that they are called to radical change is to cringe. They've experienced the pain of being excluded from a Christian group or maybe have seen how some people in the church turned their backs on those who are lost and hurting. They see this abuse of power and decide it is better to fit in with the sinners of the world who are honest about their struggles than to pretend they are somehow different from the world. We've seen some of these people get so caught up in secular culture that they use the term *Christian* only as a vague description and live as if Jesus never existed.

When Paul called us to be set apart for Christ, he wasn't concerned with titles or external appearances. He was talking about changing from the inside out as we, moment by moment, surrender to and experience Jesus's personal transformation process in our lives.

The "I have not come to call the righteous" passage from Mark exemplifies how Jesus meets us where we are. He does not expect us to get our act together before we come to Him. The path to real change is not a perfect path but a personal process. And God always seems to take that process a few steps further than we expect. Or want.

Let us give you a picture of what we mean.

LIFE REMODELED

C. S. Lewis once explained that you are like a living house and God has come to remodel you. At first He just does the little things, such as repairing holes in the roof. You knew those things needed to be fixed, so you aren't surprised by them, and you don't mind at all. But then He suddenly starts knocking out walls and making a huge mess!

"What on earth is He up to?" you ask.

You soon realize that God is doing more than a little remodeling in your life. Your life is in the middle of a major reconstruction. What you believe, how you think, what is important to you—all of it is being taken apart and put back together again. It's like God is adding new wings to the house. He's building new levels and expanding everything.

> God is doing more than a little remodeling in your life. Your life is in the middle of a major reconstruction.

He is changing everything from the inside out.

Maybe you're going through some really painful changes and challenges in your life right now, and you're not sure what God is doing. Maybe you've allowed God to come through the door of your house to start remodeling your character, but you're unsure where this will take you, or when it will end, or what your life will look like when He's finished.

When this happens to you, you're likely to be confused and full of doubts. Change, after all, is hard, and for a long time— maybe years—you won't really be able to see what God is up to. But there's a reason for it all. Lewis wrote, "You thought you were being made into a decent little cottage: but He is building a palace. He intends to come and live in it Himself." [9]

We've noticed that these times of major *internal* change often coincide with major *external* changes:

- You go off to college or graduate school.
- You travel in a different culture or live there for a while.
- You move from your small town to the big city (or the other way around).
- You suddenly face a serious health challenge.
- A relationship you deeply cared about comes to an end.

In our experience God goes to work at times like these—if we let Him. He'll find opportunities in your new, painful circumstances to transform you into a bigger, better home for Him to live in. When all you see is a life in pieces, remember: the Remodeler wants to change you from the inside out. And He's at work building your character to match His great calling and purpose for your life.

And here's the thing: *seasons of struggle and change are directly connected to getting past secondhand religion and diving deep into a vibrant, firsthand faith.* Adam from Tennessee says, "My faith reminds me that change is constant. Every day I'm presented with a choice to grow or remain stagnant. When I recognize something within me that I want to change, I know I can rely on God's strength to help me. I also know it will be a struggle, but growth comes through struggle."

When Christians in the early church were going through

terrible persecution, the apostles told them that the very best thing to come out of hard times was an unshakable faith. Here's how the apostle Peter talked about the surprising benefit of hard times: "Pure gold put in the fire comes out of it *proved* pure; genuine faith put through this suffering comes out *proved* genuine" (1 Peter 1:7, MSG).

Don't miss the payoff, Peter said. God intends for everything in your life, especially the tough times, to reshape your faith from a flimsy framework into a solid structure. *Genuine faith put through this suffering comes out proved genuine.*

This brings us to the promise of God's remodeling process. If I let Him do His work, I'll come out the other side with a firsthand faith—a relationship with God and deep, personal beliefs that are alive, authentic...and all mine.

Working with God

We'd like to suggest a couple of practices that will help you cooperate with God's process of change in your life. Of course, everyone's process will look different. And these practices are not everything you need to know for a lifetime. But they're a start.

The truth is, we don't need to have all the answers. We just need to have one or two that we're willing to put to work right now. Most of the time, that's all it takes to align ourselves with the great Remodeler's plan for our lives.

Spiritual practice 1: Be still in His presence. Our generation is in constant motion. Think about it. When was the last time you sat still for even five minutes without being in front of the TV or at the computer? We are always going from one activity to the next. And we like being on the move. Movement keeps our minds and bodies active, but it also keeps us from focusing on our souls and God's truths.

My (Ryan's) friend Sarah was one of those people who had to have her schedule filled. She was involved in several clubs, sports, extracurricular activities, and hobbies. She told me she liked being constantly on the move, but it ultimately left her exhausted and empty. "I felt fulfilled for a while," she said, "but eventually I realized I was so busy with everything that I wasn't in tune with God or His plans for me. I was exhausted at the end of every day and never felt like I was able to recharge."

In our world of constant activity, we are suffering from a certain level of motion sickness. We go from one thing to the next and never take time to catch our breath. Many Christians even think that the best path to spiritual transformation is to attend every church event or Bible study until their schedules are packed.

But God's Word tells us that if we want to be fully transformed by Him, we need the exact opposite of what our society tells us. We don't need more motion. We need less. The apostle Paul said, "Fix your attention on God" (Romans 12:2, MSG).

And the first step to fixing our attention on our Creator is to be still in His presence and experience a firsthand relationship with the God who made us. Look what God says in Psalm 46:10: "Be still, and know that I am God."

In our frantic lives, it is crucial that we stop. Not stop to watch a movie or to browse Facebook or even to talk to someone. Just stop. We are commanded to be still and to simply be in the presence of God. No more, no less. This is a discipline that sounds simple, but if you've ever tried to be still for more than a minute or so, you know it is difficult.

My (Ryan's) friend Jon explained his difficulty in learning stillness. "I sit down at the table, open up my Bible, and begin reading. After I get to the second chapter, I'm not even thinking about the words on the page! When I try to just be still and hear God's voice, my mind starts to wander. I think I've been so conditioned to keep moving and stay busy that being still feels unnatural."

Can you relate to Jon? Being still is difficult! But it's a necessary component of a truly firsthand relationship with God.

In Psalms we get a clear picture of the fulfillment that can be found in being still in God's presence. David wrote:

> He makes me lie down in green pastures,
> he leads me beside quiet waters,
> he restores my soul. (Psalm 23:2–3)

Stillness with God invites soul-deep changes. Stillness makes us new again where it really matters.

Stillness makes us new again where it really matters.

Why don't you take a moment to practice being still right now? Mark your place in the book, and set it down.

Take a deep breath, clear your mind, and close your eyes.

For one minute, stay still with your eyes closed.

In your mind see yourself lying down in green pastures or sitting quietly beside still waters.

Be aware that Christ is with you in that quiet place, and He is giving you His peace.

If you kept reading and didn't take a moment to pause, then set a time to reread these simple steps and give it a try. We encourage you to set aside five minutes every morning just to be still. What do you do for those five minutes? You can pray if you want, but we challenge you simply to focus on one of God's character qualities or on being in the presence of Christ.

As difficult as this simple discipline might be, it can be life changing. Anyone who wants to know God firsthand needs to be still before Him regularly.

Spiritual practice 2: Let God be in charge. Another major obstacle we've discovered in our lives is our constant unwillingness to give control over to God. Everyone struggles with control issues on some level. This is a struggle we need to lose.

Whenever our family would pile into our Suburban for a vacation, the entire ride would be a battle for control of the stereo. Here's a typical scenario: Our sister and mom would want to listen to classical music so they could relax. Our dad would soon try to switch the stereo over to sports radio. And Josh and I would eventually climb up to the front of the car so we could put in our Switchfoot CD. What started out as a small power struggle could quickly turn into an argument or lengthy negotiations.

It's a silly example, but maybe you can relate to this control struggle in your own spiritual walk. You feel that God is asking you not to worry about things, that He's saying He will take care of them and you only need to look for His guidance. But somehow you feel the worrying is all up to you.

I've often felt the Lord leading me to trust Him, but my initial reaction is always to hold on tighter to my control over the problem. Of course, I rationalize my reluctance to give my problem to God. *God doesn't see the whole picture on my problem,* I tell myself. *This part of my life is so insignificant to Him that He should just let me worry about it.* Other times I become impatient with God's timing. *Obviously, He isn't taking care of matters, so I need to!*

Does any of this sound familiar to you? My logic sounds ridiculous when I write it down here on the page, but all too often that's the way my mind works.

If God really is as big as He says He is, and He really does care about every detail of our lives, why is it so hard to let go of the things that matter to us and allow Him to take control?

Jesus once asked His disciples, "Who do people say I am?" (Mark 8:27).

The disciples replied, "Some say John the Baptist; others say Elijah; and still others, one of the prophets" (verse 28).

Then Jesus hit them with a question that cut right to the heart of what we're talking about here: "But what about you? Who do you say I am?" (verse 29).

Maybe your parents and your friends think God is big enough to handle all your problems. My point is that it really doesn't matter what anyone else thinks God is capable of. The question is, Who do *you* think Christ is? Is He a distant force or being who vaguely cares about you? Or is He your Creator who cares so much about you that He sacrificed His Son so He could have a firsthand relationship with you? Only you can answer that question for yourself.

All In

One of my (Ryan's) favorite verses is from Isaiah:

> This is what the Sovereign LORD, the Holy One of Israel, says:
>
> "In repentance and rest is your salvation,
>   in quietness and trust is your strength." (30:15)

Our strength comes from trusting God with our weaknesses. To be radically transformed by Christ's love, we must stop trusting in ourselves to take care of everything in our lives. He doesn't force us to let go. He asks us and waits patiently for us to trust Him. But He cannot begin transforming our lives until we admit we have a control problem and we hand the problem over to Him instead of relying on our own power.

For me, this is a daily struggle. I start the day telling God how much I need Him and acknowledging His control. Only minutes later I'm trying to figure out a problem through my own wisdom, trying to handle a situation that seems out of control, or relying completely on my strength to get through the day. I may acknowledge God with my mouth, but I often function as if I were an atheist. Can you relate?

Fortunately, God loves me so much that He allows me to fall on my face until I finally give in to His care and control. He picks me up and holds me and fills me with His strength, wisdom, and peace. And He'll do the same for you.

What real change so often comes down to is this daily surrendering to God and letting Him do whatever He wants in my life. Real change doesn't hinge on a four-part plan or five easy steps. More often it's a daily decision followed by a continual process in which I allow God to restore and remake my life one day at a time.

Looking back, I see that after I made the decision to let

Christ in the door of my life, I went a number of years without allowing Him to change and rearrange everything in my life. I let just enough God in so that I could feel better about things... but still be in control. I wasn't all in with God. My faith was definitely more about religion than relationship.

Firsthand faith is different. It's all about letting God do what He wants to in my life daily. For some reason I thought I could pray to receive Christ and then everything would fall into place. But accepting Christ is just the beginning. You can't rely on God partly and try to rely on your own strength at the same time. In the Christian life there is no hedging your bets. You're either all in with God, or you're all out. To constantly rely on your own strength while acknowledging Christ as your Savior is a contradiction that God refuses to let you get away with for very long.

> You can't rely on God partly and try to rely on your own strength at the same time.

To Act Changed or to Really Be Changed

We started out this chapter with the myth of the "happily ever after" Christian life that's common in some religious circles. The weird thing is, some people want that myth to be true so badly that they act as if they really are living "happily ever after," as if they've got it all together and everything is completely perfect in their little Christian worlds.

One of our favorite parables in the Bible cuts right through that superficiality. Jesus used this parable to teach some religious leaders about the difference between real firsthand change and fake secondhand religion. Here's how it starts:

> Two men went up to the temple to pray, one a Pharisee and the other a tax collector. The Pharisee stood up and prayed about himself: "God, I thank you that I am not like other people—robbers, evildoers, adulterers—or even like this tax collector. I fast twice a week and give a tenth of all I get." (Luke 18:10–12)

The Pharisee felt that he was a changed person because he could easily appear changed on the outside. He compared himself to the tax collector and was proud that people thought he was better than tax collectors and sinners. The truth, however, was that the Pharisee desperately needed to be changed on the inside.

It's the same today, isn't it? We can fool the people around us because they look at the outside of our lives. But Jesus Christ looks right through the surface-level appearance and straight into our messy, dark, and sinful hearts.

The Pharisee was in a more desperate situation than the tax collector, because the Pharisee didn't realize how desperate his situation really was. The tax collector, on the other hand, knew he needed change: "But the tax collector stood at a distance. He would not even look up to heaven, but beat his breast and said, 'God, have mercy on me, a sinner' " (verse 13).

Jesus went on to make His point perfectly clear to His listeners: "I tell you that this man, rather than the other, went home justified before God. For everyone who exalts himself will be humbled, and he who humbles himself will be exalted" (verse 14).

The Pharisee settled for *appearing* changed, while the tax collector wouldn't settle for anything but *real* change.

We have to decide, moment by moment, if we want to *act* changed or *be* changed. You know by now which option goes with having firsthand faith. The essence of a secondhand faith handed down from a Christian family, church, or friends is just to *act* changed. Having a firsthand faith requires the *real thing* when it comes to change. And that's why firsthand faith doesn't come easy or all at once.

We hope you feel like us and you're worn out from trying to keep up appearances. If you are, we want you to know something very important: *you are in a very promising place!* Nothing gets in God's way more than our false pride and smug religiosity. Putting down your efforts to be someone you're not and then asking God to work in your life will be one of the most important change moments of your whole life. You'll never regret it.

WORD OF THE WEEK

The Subject: God ordains certain men to hell on purpose

<u>Isaiah 64:8</u> - O Lord, thou art our Father; we are the clay; and thou our potter; and we all are the <u>work</u> of thy hand.

> <u>work</u> - Hebrew: Maaseh-an action (good or bad); product; transaction; business

<u>Romans 9:20-23</u> - Who art thou that repliest against God? Shall the thing formed say to him that formed it, why hast thou made me thus? Hath not the potter the power over the clay of the same lump, to make one vessel unto honour and another unto dishonour -- What if God willing to show his wrath, and to make his power known, endured with much long suffering the vessels of wrath fitted to destruction: And that he might make known the riches of his glory on the vessels of mercy, which he hath afore prepared unto glory.

> <u>fitted</u> - Greek: katartizo - to complete thoroughly; fit; frame; arrange; prepare. Thayer says this word speaks of men whose souls God has so constituted that they cannot escape destruction; their mind is fixed that they frame themselves.

Men get angry to think that we serve a God that can do as it pleases him. They actually think that an almighty God thinks the way they think and that he could not possibly form-fit a vessel to hell merely to show his wrath and power. Paul said he does. Men have difficulty perceiving a God that predestinates men (Rom. 8:29) on whom he desires to show his grace (unmerited favor) and mercy, that he may shower them throughout eternity with the riches of his glory. We like to believe that we must give him permission; if he is to operate in our hearts and minds. The Lord said, "My thoughts are not your thoughts, neither are your ways my ways. As the heavens are higher than the earth, so are my ways higher than your ways and my thoughts than your thoughts (Isaiah 55:8,9)". Our God is in the heavens: he hath done whatsoever he hath pleased (Psalms 115:3). He doeth whatsoever pleaseth him (Eccl 8:3). Thou, O Lord hast done as it pleased thee (Jonah 1:14). Whatsoever the Lord pleased, that did he in heaven, and earth, and in the seas, and in all deep places (Psalms 135:6). He does all his pleasure (Isa. 46:10; Isa. 44:24-28; Eph. 1:5,9; Philippians 2:13). It is Jesus that holds the keys to death and hell (Rev. 1:18), not Satan. God will intentionally cast these evil vessels of wrath into hell and lock them up for eternity because it is not his pleasure to draw them to him (John 6:44). This doctrine angers men, though it is taught throughout the pages of God's Holy Book. Men do not have a Biblical view of the living God when they think he is not in control of all things including the minds and hearts of all men. God is not only love to the vessels of mercy, but he is a consuming fire (Deut 4:24) upon the vessels of wrath fitted to destruction. We do not serve a God who is Superman that can only shake mountains, implode blackholes, and explode quasars. The God of the universe can harden and soften the hearts of men at will (Rom 9:18; Ezek. 36:26). He giveth not account of any of his matters (Job 33:13).

GRACE AND TRUTH MINISTRIES
P.O. Box 1109 Hendersonville, TN 37077
Jim Brown - Bible Teacher • 824-8502

Radio Broadcast -- Sat. Morn. 8am 1300 AM Dial WNQM
TV -- Mon. & Sat 10pm, Wed. & Fri. 12am Channel 176;
Tues. & Thurs. 5pm Channel 3; Thurs. 11am Channel 49

Join us for fellowship at 394 West Main Street on
Sunday Mornings @ 11:00am, Sunday Evenings @ 7:00pm,
Wednesday Evenings @ 7:00pm
Or
Watch us live via U-Stream on the web at
www.graceandtruth.net

Remember James, the drug addict I (Ryan) met at the homeless shelter? It took a while, but he finally came back to the center and joined another recovery group. Today he's doing well. He spends a lot of his time helping others, and God continues to change him and use him.

This isn't a happily ever after ending. James knows better than most of us how vulnerable he is to his own bad choices. But it is a redemptive ending. God can take our failures and make something out of them, and that's what makes James's testimony so powerful and relevant.

> Putting down your efforts to be someone you're not and then asking God to work in your life will be one of the most important change moments of your whole life.

We are all messes. We know it about ourselves. And God knows it too. But when we admit it to Him and start cooperating with His remodeling process in our lives, He starts turning our messes into something beautiful.

As crazy as it might sound, God can turn our messes into moving messages. It's our messes that He is using to lift up His message of freedom and firsthand faith.

Making It Real

Other Voices

This sounds crazy, but I read my Bible, and sometimes I think, *Wow! I am normal!* David was flawed, and this is the man God saw as one after His own heart. I look at Moses, and he was flawed, yet God chose him to lead. The Bible is full of flawed people. This shows me that God still loves me and can use me. —*Keisha from Livonia, Michigan*

We often put too much pressure on ourselves to look the part, and we can't maintain that. The pressure to look like a Christian or do the Christian thing is one of the biggest reasons people end up playing at Christianity. You shouldn't have to worry about what people might think or say about a place you go or a thing you do if your heart is in line with God's Word. —*Heather from Huntsville, Alabama*

We can work to change the outside, but it is all temporary. It's like putting clothing and makeup on. You can dress up and try to be all fancy, but the change is temporary. It all comes off at the end of the day. Real change starts on the inside and works out. We can't change ourselves (really). But God can. —*Kimberly from Butner, North Carolina*

I am never truly alone. Christ is always with me, constantly shaping me and nudging me to become more like Him. With that in mind, there is no such thing as "behind closed doors." As temptation creeps up, I quickly remind myself that I am not alone. I have gotten in the habit of saying the Lord's Prayer. It has really helped to realign me with Christ! —*Seth from Des Moines, Iowa*

Think About It

1. Do you ever feel pressure to hide the messes in your life and make your life look better than it is? If so, how and why?

2. What has fake religion cost you or someone you know? How could striving for real faith benefit you?

3. Have you tried spending time in stillness before the Lord? What do you like or dislike about that kind of experience?

4. In what areas of your life is it hardest for you to give control over to God?

5. Are you ready to turn away from faking a happily-ever-after faith? If so, what do you need to change in your life today?

Might Try This

● **Watch the film *Control*.**

Go to FirsthandBook.com/Control and watch Ryan's short film *Control*. Ask a friend to watch it with you. Then talk together about your reactions to it.

● **Get real with others.**

Make a positive effort to tell someone else about your failings and weaknesses. It's up to you how you want to do this. Maybe you need to apologize to others for having been a fake in front of them.

● **Have a retreat at home.**

Usually we think of summer camp or a retreat at a conference center or other special events like these as opportunities to get especially close to God. But instead, set aside time at home (or in a park or some other quiet place at hand) to be still before God. Here are a couple of suggested activities:

Identify where you're a control freak. Write down three areas of your life where you struggle to trust God and where you spend the most time and energy trying to stay in control. It could be money, a relationship, a worry, a hobby, or an addiction. If you don't want God to touch it, that's a sure indicator you are fighting to control that area. We are all control freaks in one area or another.

Take money, for example. Whether we have a little or a lot, money has to be one of the most common struggles for control that our generation suffers from. How many times have you heard, "It's my money, and I'll use it the way I want"? I hear myself saying it all the time!

For each area try to identify why it matters so much to you, what you will lose if things don't go the way you want, and how you think your loving Father might feel about what you've written.

Give it up. I invite you to close your eyes. With your eyes closed, open your hands and lay bare before Christ those people or things or behaviors you want so much to hold on to. One at a time present each area to God. Your open hands say to God, "I know You care about me much more than I care about myself." They symbolize your willingness to give to Him the things that are precious to you.

What might giving your money over to God look like? I challenge you to faithfully give to church 10 percent of whatever you make. It's not just a good idea; it's what Christ asks of us. But, more important, it teaches us to continually let go of our money and realize that God will take care of us.

As you give these things one at a time to God, ask Him

to constantly remind you that He is in control of the entire universe.

● Fight spiritual hypocrisy.

Read Matthew 6:1–18, a part of the Sermon on the Mount where Jesus contrasts fake faith with real faith in three areas (giving, praying, fasting). What ideas do these verses give you about how you can live in such a way that you aren't trying to impress others but instead are trying to please God?

● Pray.

If you want a more authentic relationship with God, tell Him about that, asking forgiveness for the ways you've been a spiritual poser and committing to follow His lead (as He gives you grace to do so) from here on.

5

Trashing the Checklist

A Faith Focused on Relationship

What were we made for? To know
God. What aim should we have in
life? To know God. What is the
eternal life that Jesus gives? To know
God. What is the best thing in life?
To know God.

—J. I. Packer

It is more important to live one word
of Scripture than it is to memorize
volumes.

—Tim Hansel

After coming back from high school church camp, I (Ryan) was determined to keep the passion I had for Christ going after summer ended and the school year began. I wrote out a list of things I was definitely going to do every single day for the rest of the year. Every day I was going to read the daily passages in a one-year Bible, pray for thirty minutes, and write at least one page in a prayer journal. Furthermore, once a week I was going to share my faith with a different person. I just knew that I would be right up there with Mother Teresa and Billy Graham by the end of the year!

By the end of the first week, I had read my Bible only once, had prayed just a few times before I ate dinner, and hadn't even invited anyone to come to church. By the time school started again, I was right back in my routine of virtually ignoring God. Whenever I was reminded of my failure to read my Bible or pray, I felt the heaviness of shame. Then my shame turned to disillusionment, and I started blaming God for being distant.

The checklist was supposed to supercharge my faith, not stifle it. What went wrong?

After camp my intentions were good. What I didn't have was a solid relationship that could serve as a foundation for my spiritual discipline. The checklist on its own made things worse, not better. What a mess!

Christ came to remove the burden of secondhand religion with all its detailed to-do lists and to bring us into a simple, real relationship. That's why when the Christians in Corinth started to add religiosity to their faith, the apostle Paul gave them a strong warning that we need today: "I am afraid that, as the serpent deceived Eve by his craftiness, your minds will be led astray from the simplicity and purity of devotion to Christ" (2 Corinthians 11:3, NASB).

Did you catch that? Paul was saying that the Christian life is not complicated. It's actually very simple. Paul told believers to get back to the simple relationship with Jesus that had changed their lives in the first place and to trash prideful, complicated religion.

For first-century Christians, religion involved overlaying countless requirements from the laws of Moses and the Old Testament on top of their new lives in Jesus. (To get an idea of all the rules they were trying to follow, check out the book of Numbers.)

For us, that sort of works-based religiosity looks like a "good Christian checklist." The list is complicated...and long...and impossible to follow without messing up.

If you grew up in church or have spent much time in one, as we have, you probably have this kind of checklist posted somewhere in the back of your brain too. Your to-do list tells you how to fit in around other Christians, how to behave around the pastor, what music you should like, and how many times a day or week you should read your Bible or pray before meals.

Of course, there's nothing wrong with caring enough about your faith to take your actions seriously. Faith that doesn't change what you do is not faith at all. But how do you separate out all the ego-boosting, people-pleasing requirements that *look* like firsthand faith but have nothing to do with the real thing?

That's what this chapter is about. This conversation is hugely important for everyone who wants to get to the heart of a living relationship with Jesus.

Simple Is Beautiful

We love the quote at the top of this chapter from the well-known theologian J. I. Packer. It's as if he's circling firsthand faith, defining it in different ways. He says it's what we're made for, what we should aim for in life. He says it's all about the eternal life we have in Jesus. It's…the best thing in life.

And what does everything that matters boil down to? Not a book-length essay on every possible way to be religious. And not a checklist of what I have to do today to be in good standing with God.

It all boils down to one thing: knowing God. *That* is firsthand faith!

When we, out of pride, mistake our checklist of "good church kid" dos and don'ts for faith itself, everything falls apart. Really, it all comes down to a love relationship with the God who created us. How can we make it any more powerful than that? Just think about the absurdity of that question! The God who put the stars in space and created in an instant the infinite universe wants to be our closest friend! That's a powerful and profound truth.

> It all comes down to a love relationship with the God who created us.

When my (Ryan's) checklist started defining my Christianity, my faith lost all its depth and power, and I lost all my joy. My faith looked healthy from the outside, but in reality I was living out a secondhand religion that was empty and lifeless.

I knew Christ died for my sins, and I had accepted His free gift of forgiveness, but beyond that I never really understood why He did it. The crazy truth is that Jesus didn't die for your sins so you could get a free pass into heaven; that was really just a bonus. The real reason that God became a man and lived a perfect life and died a brutal death was to begin an intimate and real relationship with you that lasts for eternity. That is so different from any sort of spiritual checklist!

A young woman named Rebecca from Southern California

told us that when she was a teenager, she was "the queen and model of a good, godly girl." Her friends' parents would actually invite her over to their houses so that her clean-cut behavior might rub off on their own girls. Needless to say, this didn't exactly make her popular with her peers.

Then she went to a missions camp. When the time came for her to share her faith with some young boys and girls, she emotionally shut down. She just couldn't do it. She realized she didn't have a living faith to share with anybody else.

Back home, Rebecca started backing out of church commitments. Under the circumstances it all seemed so hypocritical. Meanwhile, though, God was working in her heart.

"I realized how stuck up and annoying I had been to the people around me, but most of all to God," she says. "I had been flaunting the praise given to me in God's face. And I was wrong. I am still living with the effects of those damaged relationships, but, Lord willing, He can make good come out of my failures, no matter how bad."

Does Rebecca's story resonate with you? If so, you know that getting caught on the performance treadmill is exhausting—and doesn't get you anywhere.

Christ didn't die for you so He could make a deal with you or so He could make you follow His rules. He died to be with you. He loved you so much and so deeply that He did whatever it took to be with you.

Not until you begin to grasp the real reason for Christ's sacrifice on the cross does a firsthand faith make any sense.

BUILT ON LOVE

Regardless of how long you've been a Christian, it can be easy to lose sight of the true reason for God's sacrifice. We begin to shift our focus from the intimate relationship that God intended by His sacrifice and try to make His gift of salvation about legalism. Whether out of habit or guilt, Christians often revert to a legalistic mind-set built around rules instead of a vibrant and beautiful relationship built on love. It's exactly the kind of thing that Jesus chewed out the Pharisees for (Matthew 15:1–20; Luke 11:37–52).

Rules and discipline are important, but when they suck the life out of a relationship, they can become destructive. Many of our friends have turned their backs on Christianity because they've burned out trying to be "good Christians." They traded their intimacy with Christ for a checklist, and they lost sight of the love that brought them to Christ in the first place.

Once you make a relationship all about rules, it becomes almost impossible to derive joy from it. Spending time talking with God becomes not a pleasure but a chore. Going to church feels like a waste of time instead of an exciting celebration. Sharing your faith with friends turns into a burden, not an adventuresome risk. Maybe you're feeling the weight of legalistic Christianity in your life. Maybe you've stopped trying to grow spiritually or to connect with God in any meaningful way because you are bitter toward Him. Or maybe the relationship you once had with Christ now feels distant or even dead.

> Once you make a relationship all about rules, it becomes almost impossible to derive joy from it.

We know God loves us, but we often have difficulty delighting in Him. We find ourselves getting stuck in the motions of legalism and experiencing little joy in the presence of God. How do you rediscover delight in a relationship that feels like a dead end?

That's what Anthony from Lexington, Kentucky, was wondering. He told us, "Showing up for church all the time; being the best at Bible Bowl; leading prayer for my sports teams; going to youth rallies, FCA, Christian student events—all the things that a good Christian kid would do, I did. But I have learned that doing those things without really wanting to know and serve God is like showing up for dinner but not eating. There is no nourishment for the body, and pretty soon the body is going to wither and die."

An unnourishing meal—that's the legalistic approach to

faith. And it's unsatisfying too. Sooner or later you realize you're hungry for something better.

We don't have a ten-step plan to the perfect Christian life, but we would like to share four principles that have helped free us from checklist religion and reconnect and recharge our relationship with Christ.

OPEN THE CONVERSATION

The first step to finding the joy in your relationship with God is conversation.

Jon is one of my (Ryan's) longtime friends. He's someone I call often, and I really enjoy our conversations about shared interests and passions. We often chat about sports, work, relationships, and just about everything else that goes on in our lives. A few years back, though, I got into an argument with Jon, and we stopped talking to each other for about a month. I can't even remember what I was originally angry about, but I do remember letting our conversation die off.

Dead silence, not delight, followed. Weeks of it.

Life got busy, and other things took priority over connecting with one of my best friends. During that time it wasn't fun to think about hanging out with Jon, much less apologizing. It wasn't until weeks later that one of us picked up the phone and deliberately opened the lines of communication. As soon as we apologized and reconciled, we both started to again enjoy our friendship.

I tell you this story, not because I'm concerned about your having open communication with your friends (although that is important), but because I want you to have open communication with God. It's the same dynamic. Your relationship with Him isn't going anywhere if you're not talking to Him. And if you've been stuck in a secondhand faith, the chances are good that your prayer times are few and forced.

> Your relationship with God isn't going anywhere if you're not talking to Him.

Maybe you had an enjoyable relationship with God at one point but you've let the lines of communication shut down. Maybe you've let guilt or disappointment or busyness come between you. Whatever the situation may be, I challenge you to put down this book for five minutes and just talk with God. Talk about what's come between you. Talk about whatever you want, but be deliberate about reconnecting with Him.

By doing this, you've taken your first step away from the to-do lists and back toward enjoying your life with God.

DELIGHT IN YOUR DESIGN

One of the most amazing things about people is how different we all are. The two of us are both artistic, but we express our creativity in different ways. One of us is a musician; the other is a filmmaker. And you're different from both of us. And different from everyone you live, work, or study with.

Each of us on this planet is unique by God's design. Yet somehow—perhaps because we live in a standardized and industrialized world—it's easy to believe we are all the same or at least very similar. And this causes big problems when it comes to knowing God.

We think that one-size-fits-all assumptions keep huge numbers of Christ followers unhappy in church. Or completely outside of it. People think they have to act in a certain approved way (there's the checklist again) in order to serve God acceptably. And who wants to get stuck with that kind of uniformity? The truth, we believe, is that God put the desire for relationship in all of us but designed each of us to express that desire in unique ways.

> God put the desire for relationship in all of us but designed each of us to express that desire in unique ways.

Let me (Ryan) give you an example of how personal differences affect the way two people choose to be close to God. My wife loves to sing praises in church. It's one of the most intimate and passionate parts of her relationship with Christ. Now, I love music, but I'm more likely to feel that I am spending time with

God when I am hiking in the mountains near our home in California. When I walk through beautiful terrain on a crisp morning, I delight in God's presence and how He made me.

Maybe you find delight in God when you read the book of Psalms or engage in a favorite hobby. You were made to be unique, so your passions and approach to your relationship with God are going to be different from mine and those of the people around you. That doesn't mean you can't get close to God if you don't love singing or hiking, but it does help explain why that intimacy and delight in God is hard to find at times.

We challenge you to discover what brings *you* close to God. Identify the activities you enjoy and try doing them with the intention of talking with God. If you hate the idea of being outside for more than a few minutes, then it's probably safe to say that's not how you're going to get close to God. See what works for you, and ask God for His guidance.

God longs to be viewed not as a distant acquaintance but as a close friend. If your relationship with Him has lost momentum, then God doesn't want you to kill yourself trying to complete a checklist of good spiritual disciplines. As in any meaningful relationship, there comes a point when you have to pause and focus on what truly matters. And being with Him, delighting in Him—*knowing* Him—is what matters most.

That's why we challenge you to dump those one-size-fits-all assumptions that checklist religion is always based on. Forget about following the rules for now, and instead try rediscovering what first brought you joy in your relationship with Christ. When you find yourself delighting in your relationship with God, you are forming a firsthand bond that will be stronger than any checklist could ever produce.

MOVE FROM BIBLE READING TO BIBLE RELATIONSHIP

We're not saying to never read your Bible and stop going to church and drop all spiritual discipline. We're simply saying that we must always examine our motives to make sure we are trying to draw closer to God rather than trying to gain His approval.

Take Bible reading. Of course, we know it's essential to read the Bible and study it in order to grow closer to God, but consider a few practical ways to keep your quiet time in God's Word fresh.

Instead of trying to read several chapters a day and trying to complete a Bible reading goal, maybe pick one promising verse to read—for the next week. Read that verse, and only that verse, every day during your quiet time. Then spend a few minutes thinking about it. Meditate on it. Consider what it might mean and, given your unique design, how you could apply it to your life. Ask God to help you understand it and live it out.

I (Josh) like to read a one-year Bible, which has a reading plan that takes me through the Bible in a year. But I have found I try so hard to keep up with the required reading that I don't take time to soak in the truth.

Someone said the Bible was not written to increase our knowledge; it was written to change our lives. Don't miss Tim Hansel's powerful statement at the top of this chapter: "It is more important to live one word of Scripture than it is to memorize volumes." Most of us could probably read the same verse for a year and *still* not completely integrate its truths into our lives.

I'm not so bothered now when I get behind in my one-year Bible. If I let it change me as I go, I don't think God cares if it takes me ten years to read through the Bible. He just wants me to encounter Him in such a way that it changes my character.

Maybe someone should put together a ten-year Bible, but I'm afraid no Christian would buy it. We would be too afraid someone might see us buying it and think: *Wow. That guy sure isn't very spiritual. He's buying a ten-year Bible.* The way some Christians talk about their relationship with Christ, you'd think they'd just finished the one-week Bible!

The point I'm trying to make is that, even though reading and studying God's Word are essential for growing your first-hand relationship with Him, you shouldn't let the Bible become just another item on your to-do list. When you love someone, you want to spend time with her. You want to read his love letters. The reason we should develop a daily discipline of reading God's love letter is to get close to Him—not to show Him we won the competition.

It's so much more important to develop the life discipline of reading God's Word than it is to read large chunks of the Bible at a time. Don't beat yourself up if you miss a day or two or three. Remember, you're not doing it to win God's blessings and favor (that would be checklist Christianity). God loves you the same whether you spend time with Him or not. He longs for you to spend time with Him because He knows how much you need Him every day. Just ask for His free forgiveness, and get back with Him the next day.

Choose Reckless Confidence over Boring Religion

Maybe the most important action step that recharged us was taking risks in faith and experiencing the exhilaration of seeing God be real in our lives. We took to heart what Oswald Chambers said: "Faith is the heroic effort of your life; you fling yourself in reckless confidence on God. God has ventured all in Jesus Christ to save us, now He wants us to venture our all in abandoned confidence in Him."[10]

Firsthand faith requires that each of us constantly take risks in faith to obey God. We think Oswald Chambers would call firsthand faith a faith of "reckless confidence on God," one where we constantly let go of security and comfort and let God catch us and hold us.

What does reckless confidence on God look like in different people's lives?

You—and we—were made to live passionately, taking risks in faith and following God with all our hearts. But as we go through life, we naturally drift into seeking comfort and security and minimizing risks. When we do that, joy and delight go missing from our faith. But when we step out in faith and trust God, we come alive and get to see His faithfulness firsthand.

We watched our parents step out in faith and plant a church when we were boys. They had very little money at the time, just a dream God had placed on their hearts to reach the lost and hurting. They started with fifteen people, and from there it dwindled to eight after the first gathering. Five were our family! Now thousands are part of the church. But we know all the little miracles God did along the way as our parents would step out in faith and watch God come through.

We feel as though we've had front-row seats to watch God working in our parents' lives as they've taken risks in faith to obey God's call. But in a sense it's been their experience, not ours. We need our own experiences of stepping out in faith and watching God act. We don't want front-row seats anymore. We want to be in the game! We want to see God at work up close and personal in our lives.

We have to admit, one of the reasons our faith slipped into the crises we talked about at the beginning of this book was that we stopped taking our own steps of faith in reckless abandonment to God. But what is Christianity if it's not a great adventure with the God who made us? From our own experiences, we can tell you that when we stopped taking risks in faith, all we had left was boring religion.

It's different now. Both of us have graduated college and live thousands of miles from our hometown. We are pursuing our respective passions of film and music and believing God for big things. It's scary. It's exhilarating. And it's right where God wants us to be right now, trusting Him one day at a time. We feel insecure and afraid at times, but we also feel completely alive, knowing we have to trust God.

What about you?

Much more important than moving somewhere new is stepping out to take risks of faith every day to obey what God is speaking into your life. Risks like opening up to a friend who doesn't have a faith in Christ about what your faith means to you. Like going on a mission trip and getting out of your comfort zone. Like being a friend to someone who isn't in the popular crowd at school without worrying about what people think.

What adventure is calling you?

TEARING UP THE CHECKLIST

"I was looking for the magic formula that would cause God to love me," a woman named Ginny from West Virginia told us about her young adulthood. "Read the Bible—check! Do something nice today—check! Help out in the church—check! Pray—check! Tithe—check! The trouble is that none of that really made me feel closer to God; it just made me tired."

That tiredness made her stop and think. Obviously something was wrong. Ginny began to recalculate what was really supposed to go into her relationship with God. And over time she began to understand that God doesn't care so much about the checklist.

"God wants my heart, not my actions," she realized. "When my heart is right, the actions flow without effort. My 'fruits' become part of my worship rather than a list of things to accomplish today."

When our faith looks like a long list of things we should do, it's usually a sign we're not really focusing on knowing God today for ourselves. Firsthand faith is all about a relationship with the God who is always faithful. And we can't experience His faithfulness firsthand unless we let go and let Him catch us.

It's really quite simple—as simple as trusting God with everything. Of course, simple is not always easy. We'll fail many times to trust Him. We'll find ourselves complicating our faith all over again. But as we throw out checklist religion, we know that God will never, ever let us go.

Making It Real

Other Voices

I was definitely the "good girl," wanting to please the adults around me. I went through about three years of self-examination, anger, frustration, and wanting to give up. Fortunately, I had a group of godly friends who were surrounding me, helping me, and praying for me. The interesting thing was they didn't judge me. They gave me the grace to arrive at God's conclusion in God's timing—with no pressure, I might add. —*Becky from Central City, Nebraska*

I accepted Christ when I was young but put my walk with Him on the back burner around sixth grade. I didn't become serious about my walk with Christ until I got to high school. By the time I made it there, I felt like I had to do everything I could to make up for all the time I had wasted. I began going to every Bible study, going on every trip, and so on. This continued when I got into college. But no matter how much I did, I still felt like I hadn't done enough.

It wasn't until my junior year of college that I finally realized I was holding myself to a distorted view of grace. Christ's death on the cross paid the price for all my failures. The more I relied upon myself to try to get right with God, the more I pushed Christ to the background. There's nothing I can do to make up for my mistakes, but luckily I don't have to, because Christ has already made them up for me!

When I finally realized this, it was incredible how quickly the pressure seemed to lift and how much more I experienced the full, rich life that Christ came to give me! —*Patrick from Lock Haven, Pennsylvania*

I am a firstborn child as well as a high achiever and, to top it off, a pastor's daughter, so I had multiple levels of performance issues to work through. I had to wrestle with the inner belief (which was a lie) that I had to be the best in order to be valuable. It was exhausting. And in my relationship with God, I naturally thought that the harder I tried, the better Christian I would be. So I became burdened with my own expectations of a prayer life and devotional life that worked for a while but eventually burned me out. It was part of my growth in Him to move past those behaviors and to have a more relaxed relationship with Him that was full of grace. —*Justine from Coldwater, Michigan*

Think About It

1. Did you have (or do you still have) a "Christian check-list"—things you are burdened about because you feel

you *have* to do them? If so, what is on your checklist? Where do you think that list comes from?

2. What effect has checklist Christianity had on your faith?

3. What do you need to do to get rid of the checklist and get back to the joy of a relationship with God?

4. What could a checklist-free faith look like in your life?

Might Try This

● **Question your motives.**

Read Luke 10:38–42. Do you identify more with Mary or Martha in this passage? If you find yourself identifying more with Martha—so distracted by accomplishing stuff that you're not even paying attention to Jesus—then think about how you can be more like Mary and what motivated her.

● **Get advice from someone older.**

Frankly, lots of Christians out there present a bad model when it comes to checklist Christianity. But we believe that if you look hard enough, you should be able to find someone older and wiser who has survived the checklist phase and has a warm relationship with God that isn't dependent on doing certain things. If you find someone like this, then ask this person how he or she maintains a joyful relationship with Christ in spite of the pressure to keep up appearances.

● Trash your checklist—literally!

Write down on a piece of paper all the rules you can think of that you have been following as a substitute for developing a real relationship with God. Then rip it up or crumple it and put it in the trash. You may feel weird about this at first, but it could be very freeing.

● Pray.

Speak to God about your problem with checklist Christianity. Talk to Him about your struggle with it, and share your heart about how you truly want to know Him on a more intimate level.

6

Question Everything
A Faith Unafraid of Doubt

Doubt is not the opposite of faith; it is
an element of faith.

—Paul Tillich

If ours is an examined faith, we
should be unafraid to doubt. If doubt
is eventually justified, we were
believing what clearly was not worth
believing. But if doubt is answered,
our faith grows stronger still. It knows
God more certainly, and it can enjoy
God more deeply.

—Os Guinness

One of the biggest struggles in my (Ryan's) spiritual life has been the battle with doubt. As if the doubts themselves weren't enough, I used to think that to question my faith meant that I was a bad person. Sitting in church, I'd have thoughts like, *Did Jesus really rise from the dead?* When my dad would glance at me from the stage, I just knew he was reading my mind.

I'd feel immediate pangs of guilt. *Oh, God, what have I just done?* I'd think. *I am such a fraud!*

In high school I got so sick of feeling guilty about my doubts that I decided to embrace them. I'd ask my friends if they really believed the Bible was true, if they believed that God even existed. I took on the role of devil's advocate with friends, arguing that maybe nothing in the Bible was true.

Some would say that I was just trying to be controversial, and that may have been partly true. But there was something deeper going on. Something very important. And I see it more clearly now.

I was actually trying to move from beliefs that had been

handed to me by others to beliefs that I wanted to own for myself. I was trying to move from secondhand faith to firsthand faith.

And I realize now that there was no way I could detour around the hard questions and hope to arrive at a real, personal, lifelong experience of God. Most other followers of Christ I've talked to can't either. The wrestling match with doubt can be messy, scary, and painful. But in the tough parts of life, it may be unavoidable. Even better, it can be necessary, energizing, and life changing.

That's what we want to talk about in this chapter. Instead of feeling unspiritual or second-class because you're hit by questions and doubts, or instead of running away from God entirely, we want you to be able to face your doubts.

As strange as it sounds, healthy doubts often become the building blocks for a faith that lasts. That's why we like theologian Paul Tillich's statement at the top of this chapter: "Doubt is not the opposite of faith; it is an element of faith." We want to help you think about doubts differently. By the end of this chapter, we hope you'll see that doubts can actually help you get to the firsthand faith you've always wanted—an understanding and experience of God that you can get enthusiastic about, that you can rely on for the rest of your life.

Healthy doubts often become the building blocks for a faith that lasts.

HONEST TO GOD

As Tillich seems to be saying, spiritual doubts don't exist by themselves, apart from personal faith. For us, it's more like this: We believe deep in our hearts that God is going to come through for us—we really do. Then doubts creep in. Before we know it, doubts and beliefs are all mixed together. We can totally identify with the man who brought his son to Jesus to be healed, and Jesus told him that all things are possible for those who believe. The man responded by saying, "I do believe; help me overcome my unbelief!" (Mark 9:24).

I do believe; help me overcome my unbelief!

Do you ever feel that way?

The further we get on our spiritual journeys, the more grateful we are that we have been willing to honestly struggle with unbelief. You might wonder why we'd say such a thing. But we think that a blind faith is a weak faith. And the way to get away from weak faith is to bring your doubts to God in a healthy and biblical way. That man in Mark shows us exactly how to do it: simply tell God the truth. "Lord, I believe! But help me with my unbelief too!"

If we are willing to do that, good things will start to happen.

The main benefit we've found from facing doubts honestly is that the process can make faith much more personal and real. We have friends who decided to suppress their doubts, to put them out of their minds and pretend they didn't matter. Now these same friends seem to be stuck with a fake faith that doesn't have any substance, or they have given up on their faith altogether. Sure, it can be uncomfortable to wrestle with tough questions. But in our experience, faith grows stronger and gets more real when we're willing to face our doubts with open hearts.

Another good thing about facing your doubts head-on is that it allows you to talk much more freely about your faith. Your values and how you treat others will change. When I (Ryan) first became a Christian, I would look for opportunities to prove that my faith was the best. I would get into shouting matches with atheist friends about how Christianity was unquestioningly scientific fact. This arguing made me look ignorant and did nothing but turn my friends off to the idea of firsthand faith. I've overheard way too many similar shouting matches between people who claimed to be open-minded.

In order to talk honestly about my beliefs and doubts with others, I've had to mature. When you accept that you may never be able to prove your faith 100 percent scientifically, you're forced to drop your pride and smug self-satisfaction. You learn to listen more carefully and respectfully to the thoughts and feelings of others. If the Christians who are always looking for a religious fight really understood this, our faith would be better off.

When I speak honestly about my doubts to other believers, or simply to God in prayer, that act of courage opens up my heart to learn so much more about the power of Christian fellowship and the truth of God's character. I've never been the kid at the front of the class with all the answers, but I have often been the equally annoying kid at the back of the class with all the questions. I've always believed that "if you don't ask, you won't know." God wants us to ask Him questions. You may not come away from a discussion on doubts with a tweetable one-liner, but I guarantee that when you ask honest questions, you will ultimately learn something about God's character or yourself or both.

It was a huge breakthrough for me when I realized that God wasn't disgusted or angry with me because I had doubts. You and I can tackle our doubts and fears with a deeply reassuring confidence that God is with us on our journey. He's not upset or annoyed by our questions. He doesn't think we're disloyal or ungrateful brats. Rather, He is pleased that we care enough to ask, to wonder, to dig deeper.

Of course, people have been voicing doubts about faith for centuries, and we all have countless questions. But Josh and I want to focus on three main doubts about God that most Christians have struggled with at some time—doubts about where God is, what He is doing, and what He is capable of.

"God, Where Are You?"

One day when I (Ryan) was eight, I went to the mall with my mom to get some clothes. After wading through the clothes department aisles for what felt like forever, I spotted the video game section mere feet away. Before I could even think twice, my feet were moving toward the game displayed on the TVs. When I turned around a few minutes later to find my mom, I realized I had lost her. I ran around the store as quickly as my chubby legs could take me, my eyes darting from aisle to aisle, hoping I would catch a glimpse of Mom. But she was nowhere to be found.

The knot in my stomach tightened as reality set in. I would never see my mom or family again. I was an orphan now. All hope was lost.

But hope wasn't lost. Sure, I was *convinced* Mom had vanished—until she suddenly appeared and said, casual as can be, "Hey, where'd you go?" She had never been very far away. She was just out of my sight.

Have you ever found yourself wondering where God is? Maybe you have found yourself asking the question in a stressful or disastrous situation. Maybe you've been struck with an overwhelmingly emotional feeling that God has left you. Maybe a nagging question has grown in the back of your mind over time.

God, where are You?

We think that behind the "Where are You?" question often lies a more fundamental one: "*Who* are You?"

Are You good?

Are You trustworthy?

Do You care?

Everywhere you look in the world around you there seems to be injustice, environmental degradation, and human suffering. You're not alone if you can't help wondering whether God just left us to rot. What should a thoughtful person do when faced with the realities of a painful and often unfair world?

One of the people we talked to—Brian from Oregon—told us, "I have been struggling with a lot of job issues and am starting to question whether I should keep doing this or not. I just feel hopeless and empty. It is sad to say, but at times I feel like God has left me behind."

Feeling left behind. Like me in the department store.

We love the passion with which the author of Psalm 10 pours out his heart when faced with the seeming absence of God. "Why, O LORD, do you stand far off?" he wrote. "Why do you hide yourself in times of trouble?" (verse 1). The author of this psalm was doing exactly what God wants us to do when faced with doubts about His presence. He didn't bury his doubts. And he didn't just complain about his doubts to his friends. Instead, he brought his doubts directly to God.

We believe that kind of brutal honesty with God is always the first step you need to take with your doubts. Think about this: God is no less with you in your doubts than He is with you in your certainties. No difference. In the middle of your doubts,

God hasn't moved, and He hasn't disappeared. At the moment maybe you can't see or feel Him, but just because you're doubting doesn't mean He's not still there.

> God is no less with you in your doubts than
> He is with you in your certainties.

During an especially hard time in Israel's history, God seemed so far away that the people wondered if He'd left them to waste away in their sins. They looked around at their disastrous circumstances and came to the conclusion that they'd finally pushed God too far. He was done with them. He was going to let them fend for themselves.

But God told the prophet Jeremiah to pass on to His people this unshakable promise about His nearness: "You will seek me and find me when you seek me with all your heart" (Jeremiah 29:13).

God has things He can teach us while He's seemingly MIA and we're wandering about or feeling abandoned. And meanwhile He's still there. In the end He will make sure we find Him again. Like the Israelites, you may be in a place right now where you feel that God has abandoned you. We don't know how long that feeling will last, but we want to remind you that God does not abandon His daughters and sons. Keep seeking Him, keep praying, and don't give up!

But even if you are sure God is there, you may find yourself facing another area of confusion and doubt.

"God, What Are You Doing?"

How many times have you found yourself praying that God would act? "Do something!" we cry out. "Change this! And please, Lord...do it now!"

I (Ryan) have to admit that I am always asking God to do something for me or to give something to me. Then when things don't work out as I had hoped and prayed, I get angry and frustrated. I doubt God's purpose for my life. I jump to conclusions like *If God really loved me, He would have helped me get that job!* Or kept me healthy. Or sent me money.

It's embarrassing to admit, but I've found that it's easy to doubt God's actions when they don't line up with my plans. Can you relate? But that logic doesn't hold up. No, God's plans and ours don't always mesh, but that doesn't mean He doesn't know and care about what is best for us.

I guess it's a maturity thing. As a teenager, I would get furious when my parents wouldn't let me go out with friends on a school night or wouldn't give me more money when I wanted to buy something. I would bitterly insist that my mom and dad didn't really care about me. If they did, they would act differently.

Right?

But looking back, I can see how much my parents really did love me. They weren't trying to ruin my life; they just cared enough to try to save me from bad influences or greed or some other harm. I'm so thankful they kept me from making some really dumb mistakes and instead let me get upset about what "terrible" parents they were.

In the same way, we may never fully understand or agree with God's plan, but that doesn't mean He is not at work for our good.

> We may never fully understand or agree with God's plan, but that doesn't mean He is not at work for our good.

When my wife and I first moved to Los Angeles, we were confused by all the roads and highways. It would take us hours to find our way across town as we merged onto and off highways and ended up taking wrong turn after wrong turn. We'd comment to each other, "What were the city planners thinking when they decided to make this road dead-end here and start again five blocks later?"

Without a doubt you'll experience times when it looks as if God is toying with your life. But He knows more than you do, and He loves you more than you even love yourself.

As you journey through life, there will be dead ends, U-turns, and frustrating one-way streets. Not to mention traffic jams that leave you at a standstill.

A woman named Elizabeth from Columbus, Ohio, told us she began to question God's intentions when it came time to plan her future after graduation. She recalled, "He didn't seem to be moving fast enough or speaking clearly enough. Did He really have a purpose for me? What if I trusted Him and His plans weren't worth it?"

The time seemed to drag on and on, and she didn't know where God was leading her—if He was leading her at all.

And it really got to her.

"I started clawing for control," she said, "trying to ensure I wouldn't fail or flop. And then it was too much for me. I became anxious, irritable, and out of control."

She eventually found some reassurance in Scripture that she didn't have to trust in her own understanding. She read in Jeremiah 29:11: " 'I know the plans I have for you,' declares the LORD, 'plans to prosper you and not to harm you, plans to give you hope and a future.' " Obviously this didn't clarify everything about her postgraduation future. But it taught her to trust the Plan Maker.

Like Elizabeth, you can choose to get angry, to fight what appears to be illogical and senseless planning on God's part, to try to take control. I know I have. I am always looking for the next big thing that I want out of life. Not until I get that thing do I realize I completely missed out on the journey because I didn't take the time to enjoy it. Over time, though, I've found it's easier to keep a joyful heart when I remember my final destination and who is really in control of my life.

Our souls are eternal, and God made us to be with Him forever. If we think our final destination in the journey of life is supposed to be living in a big mansion with a gigantic TV and the most expensive car, then we will always doubt God when His plan doesn't seem to work around our plans. But God has bigger and longer lasting things in mind for us than we can even imagine. And because God exists in the past, present, and future and He knows exactly what we need, He may not give us that thing we wanted, but He will always give us what we really need (Romans 8:28–30).

Maybe you're sure that God has plans for you and His plans are good. But what if you're really struggling to believe that God will come through for you? How do you deal with doubt about God's power?

"GOD, CAN YOU HANDLE THIS?"

When we were kids, we believed our dad was the strongest man on earth. We would team up on Dad and try to take him down. We'd jump on his back, climb up his arms, wrap ourselves around his legs—whatever we could think of to try to bring him to his knees.

Never worked, though. We barely got him to budge.

Of course, back then we were small, and our perspective was limited. Dad really *is* a strong guy, but the strongest man on earth? No. Sorry, Dad. Definitely not. Now that we're older, we see things differently.

Maybe you've had a change of perspective about God. When you were young or first became a Christian, you believed God could do anything, but now you doubt He can or will.

How do you reconcile the terrible evil in the world with a loving God who is strong enough to make a difference? Or to bring it down to a more personal level, if He is all-powerful, why won't He take away just one of your stupid sin habits when you ask Him to?

These kinds of questions have plagued God's people forever. Listen to the worship leader Asaph pour out his frustration:

How long will the enemy mock you, O God?
    Will the foe revile your name forever?
Why do you hold back your hand, your right
        hand? (Psalm 74:10–11)

There's something about a good superhero movie that I (Ryan) love. Maybe it's the clear distinction between good and evil or the way the superheroes face certain defeat but somehow always beat the odds to claim victory over the bad guys. (Maybe it's just because I love explosions and wish I could fly.) But I think there's more to it. Something about these stories resonates deep inside us. We all want to see love conquer hate. We all wish things could be made right as soon as possible.

Of course, even in the best superhero movies, good never beats evil right away. In fact, it usually takes a few sequels—and maybe a prequel—for the good guys to triumph.

This story-line approach to understanding God's actions in this world has helped me a lot. The Bible tells us where the story started and where it will end. But right now we live in the in-between. Our world is a place of tension where evil still exists and where, even though the superhero has arrived on the scene, the battle rages on. We see the battle in our own lives and in our own hearts. No wonder we often feel an overwhelming tension that can make us just want to give up.

> The Bible tells us where the story started and where it will end. But right now we live in the in-between.

That's how Wendi from Orange County, California, felt.

Wendi was raised as a Christian in a supposedly Christian home. Yet all the while she was being molested by her "Christian" grandfather. She felt conflicted by the contradiction between her religious upbringing and the facts of the real world. *If God loves me and is all-powerful,* she thought, *why doesn't He stop this? I must not be worth His time.*

When she became a teenager, she told her parents about the abuse, believing her grandfather might molest another child if she didn't tell them. Not long after, her grandfather—having heard about what she'd said—called her on the phone and blamed all the years of abuse on her. To Wendi, this was confirmation that God was not for her.

She spent the next several years angry with God. She believed He was real; she just didn't want anything to do with Him. But still she kept up a mental dialogue with Him over the years.

Then in her midtwenties she was caught in a flash flood. When a car—carried along by the floodwaters—crashed through the living room wall of the house she was in, she escaped with several friends just in time to scramble up a huge boulder. There they sat, huddled together, and watched the rain-soaked mountainside sliding down. It took everything in its path, including people trying to run out of their homes just as they had done. Wendi and her friends thought they were going to die too.

In this crisis Wendi finally cried out to God—the same God she had denied and fought with for years. And His answer to her was immediate.

"I can tell you without hesitation," she said, "that I have never in my life felt such overwhelming peace. In the moment before my certain death, Jesus wrapped His arms around me and gave me a calmness you cannot imagine, and I surrendered to Him with everything I had at that moment. I chose Christ, who had chosen me all along."

Wendi survived the flooding and the mud slide. Her renewed faith in Christ survived too. Survived and flourished.

Looking back later, she concluded that she needed the years of struggle and pain to appreciate what she was missing without a firsthand faith.

"Now I am a witness that cannot be overlooked," she says. "A woman of experiences and challenges who can relate to others who have known pain and feelings of rejection and hopelessness. As a chaplain, Bible study leader, and disaster-relief volunteer, I have been God equipped to empathize and comfort those who would otherwise reject His love. I am truly blessed by His purpose for my life and the journey I have taken."

That's a woman who has come through doubts about God, and even dislike of Him, to a place where she has a faith that is alive and active and doing much good in the world.

Take the Step

Do you realize that everyone on earth is living by faith? Even the atheist has faith in something unprovable—in this case, the absence of God. By its very definition, faith means believing in something without having final proof or complete understanding. As we read in the book of Hebrews, "Faith is being sure of what we hope for and certain of what we do not see" (11:1).

We have faith that gravity will keep our feet on the ground instead of our floating off into space, but this is something we "do not see." We are "sure" of this belief, but do we have visible proof? Not really.

In the same way, we have reasonable evidence that leads us to believe God is good and strong and at work in our world. Still, to live out that belief, we must ultimately take a step of faith.

We've found four practical choices that help us a lot on our spiritual journeys. And we especially recommend them to any Christian who struggles with faith and doubt.

We recommend that you:

Stay in conversation with God. Although no human being has all the answers, the good news is that God gave us the Bible as our road map and the Holy Spirit as our guide to lead us to truth. We don't travel alone—that is so encouraging! God Himself will show us the light we need for our next step if we sincerely seek it.

It's okay to share your honest questions with friends and church leaders. But if all you do is voice your doubts without bringing them to God, then your faith will never be your own. When you present your doubts in prayer to God and dig into Scripture for answers, you are maintaining an open and honest dialogue with Him. You are making it easier for His Spirit and His words to speak and move in your heart.

Put your heart into your quest for the truth. Doubts may start in your head, but unless you let those questions penetrate your heart, they will always just be intellectual questions instead of what they should be—the natural growth process of a firsthand faith.

Like us, you probably know people who seem to be talking heads when it comes to questions of faith. They have plenty of opinions, questions, and quotations. They could argue one position or another for ages—and they just might. In his second letter to Timothy, Paul warned about insincere seekers who are "always learning but never able to acknowledge the truth" (2 Timothy 3:7).

That's why we recommend you bring more than your questions to God. Bring Him your heart too. And your will. And your deepest desires. He sees you as more than just an intellect. He sees you as a whole person, and He wants to reveal Himself to all of you.

Embrace the mystery of life. In an age when you can instantly research almost any question on Google, it's easy to believe there's no real mystery left in the world. But this line of thinking can be a trap. Socrates wrote, "True knowledge exists in knowing that you know nothing." Your human nature craves understanding, can't rest until every question gets answered, every fact is nailed down. But it's arrogant to think you will ever be able to understand everything.

No matter how well educated you are, there will always be

so much you don't know—about inner and outer space, about the oceans, psychology, physics, human nature, even your own body. You can let this realization of your limitations defeat you, or you can embrace the wonderful mystery of the world around you. You can and should challenge yourself to learn and understand more. But you also need to humbly acknowledge that God, your Creator, is the only One who will ever understand everything.

Have faith in God's faithfulness. When people present us with their doubts, we usually remind them that, although they may have lost faith in God, He hasn't lost faith in them. Faith is a process, and doubting is a part of human nature. When nothing else seems clear, you can have faith in God's faithfulness. The apostle Paul wrote, "What if some did not have faith? Will their lack of faith nullify God's faithfulness? Not at all!" (Romans 3:3–4).

Many of our friends still think God is going to punish them for second-guessing Him. But that's not going to happen. (Spend time with the New Testament stories of Peter and Thomas if you don't believe us.) Just because you have doubts about God does not mean that He has doubts about you!

Think about it: if you have accepted Christ into your life as your Lord and Savior, God is not going to send you to hell for a bunch of annoying questions! A question—even an irresolvable doubt—is not the same thing as totally rejecting Christ.

RESTING IN HIS PRESENCE

When I (Ryan) was very young, I never wanted to go to sleep. My parents would put me down in my bed, and I would try to keep my eyes open as long as I could. I'd make noises or look around the room as I tried hard to keep my eyelids from closing. I'm not sure why I wanted to stay awake, but I do remember my dad often holding me before bedtime. With his arms around me and my chin on his shoulder, he would gently bounce me up and down until I finally fell asleep.

Now that I'm older, I realize that I'm always fighting my faith the same way I tried to fight sleep as a child. I throw an unlimited number of doubts at God and try to stay in control of my entire world. But eventually, after I've finally worn myself out with questions and given up my struggle, God looks at me with the gentle smile of a father and simply holds me in His arms.

I don't know where you are right now in your struggle with doubt. But I know exactly where God is. At the end of the day, God is still there, ready to hold you, no matter what you think about Him or what you've said about Him.

At the end of the day, God is still there, ready to hold you, no matter what you think about Him or what you've said about Him.

God is waiting for you to experience the peace that comes from stepping back from your questions at times and simply relaxing in His arms. No matter how many questions or doubts you or I may have, we can take comfort in the fact that God is still God, He still loves us, and, ultimately, He is still in control.

Firsthand faith means that we're not afraid to bring our burning questions directly to God. But it also means that we're not afraid to simply relax in His love. Even when all our questions haven't yet been answered.

Making It Real

Other Voices

When I was younger, I was afraid to ask the really hard questions that I had. But the older I got, the more I began to realize that if Christianity is worth following and God's Word is true, then no question is too hard for God to handle. Truth will always withstand the toughest scrutiny. —*John from Spring Lake, North Carolina*

My biggest struggle was learning that partying and sex and alcohol weren't going to bring me joy and comfort and that they would only interfere with my relationship with Christ. The drinking and partying friends I made weren't really interested in hanging out with me if I wasn't partying and involved in a sinful lifestyle with them.

When I was a young Christian, I questioned many times if losing all my friends was worth it. I felt lonely. But God was faithful to bring me through it. He gave me an amazing husband and brought me to a wonderful church and provided new, Christ-honoring friends to have fellowship with. He showed me that He was with me, even in my loneliest times. —*Brenna from Panama City, Florida*

Does God really care about *me*? Seriously, every little detail of my life? I know He does, because I can look back on things and smile and realize that there is no way other than God's help that certain things in my life worked out as they did. —*Teresa from Prattville, Alabama*

I have many doubts and questions about God's ways, His justice, and who will really be saved. But I realized in college that God is not intimidated by my doubts or questions. If He really is God, my doubts and questions do not change who He is. He has proven His goodness and faithfulness to me several ways, so now I know He is trustworthy even when I don't understand what's going on in or around me. —*Curtis from Casper, Wyoming*

I think we do such a disservice to each other as Christians if we pretend we've got it all together or pretend we never doubt. I've had women in my small group confess the whispered secret, "Sometimes I doubt that God is really there." They glance around in fear of rejection, shame, or being kicked out of the group. I'm quick to reassure them that I struggle with doubts too.

I always go back to the Bible, and that helps me through my struggles. And it helps me share with others who are struggling. —*Heather from Gloucester, Virginia*

At the age of twenty, I lost my fiancé to a tragic accident. From that event came many doubts and arguments with and about God. After a time I came around to see that God had been by my side and had gifted me with an understanding beyond any of my friends or family about such horrible loss.

Soon after, a dear friend lost his young wife to cancer. Family members faced and entered heaven almost in a waiting line, it seemed, for several years in a row. A lot of loss and grief surrounded me. But through it all I was often told by other grievers that they appreciated my presence as refreshing and felt I truly knew what they were going through.

My doubt and anger had turned into a ministry. —*Kristy from Hopkins, Michigan*

Think About It

1. What do you think about the concept of doubt actually being a healthy part of your faith?

2. What has been your journey through faith and doubt since you were a child?

3. What are your biggest questions or doubts about God right now? What effect are those questions and doubts having on your faith and on your life in general?

4. What step of faith do you need to take right now to move toward God in spite of your doubts and questions?

5. Are you able to relax in God even though all your questions are not yet resolved? If so, how do you do that?

Might Try This

● **Get creative.**

Many psalms are the words of people pouring out their doubts and questions to God. Are You there? Do You still care about me? When are You going to do something about my problem?

Follow in the psalmists' footsteps, and express what you're thinking and feeling in some kind of art form. Depending on what you're good at, write a poem, come up with a short story, write a song, paint a picture, make a sculpture—whatever. It will help you process your experience and might even touch someone else's heart.

● **Track down the answers.**

There are some doubts that no one else can resolve for you (for example, *God, how could You let the love of my life get away?*).

And there are other doubts where, well, maybe there *is* an answer for you out there (for example, *Can I really believe the New Testament is reliable?*). If you're dealing with the second kind of doubt, we encourage you to look for answers.

There are lots of books and websites on the topic of Christian apologetics (which refers to defense of the faith), and you might find what you're looking for in one of them. As we said in an earlier chapter, books by Josh McDowell have really helped us. Or you can go to a study resource such as a topical Bible and start looking up passages on the subject you're interested in.

Start looking!

● **Read about a fellow doubter.**

John 20:24–29 tells the story of a man known to history as doubting Thomas. Read his story, and then ask yourself these questions:

- How is Thomas's doubt similar to mine? different from mine?
- What was Jesus's reaction to Thomas's doubt, and what does this say about Him?
- How do Jesus's words "Blessed are those who have not seen and yet have believed" apply to me?

● **Pray.**

Even if you're not totally sure that God is in heaven or really listening to your prayer, pray to Him anyway. Pour out your doubts and questions to Him—don't hold anything back. Ask Him to reveal Himself to you so that you can trust in Him for yourself, not just because others have told you that you should.

7

Divine Disturbance
A Faith Outside the Comfort Zone

Intense love does not measure; it just gives.

— Mother Teresa

The people who are crazy enough to think that they can change the world are the ones who do.

— Steve Jobs

Disturb us, Lord, when
We are too pleased with ourselves,
When our dreams have come true
Because we dreamed too little,
When we arrived safely
Because we sailed too close to the shore.

Disturb us, Lord, when
With the abundance of things we possess
We have lost our thirst
For the waters of life;
Having fallen in love with life,
We have ceased to dream of eternity
And in our efforts to build a new earth,
We have allowed our vision
Of the new Heaven to dim.

Disturb us, Lord, to dare more boldly,
To venture on wilder seas
Where storms will show Your mastery;
Where losing sight of land,
We shall find the stars.

This poem is thought to have been written by Sir Francis Drake, the famous sixteenth-century adventurer. That makes it hundreds of years old. But even today I (Josh) feel like this poem is the continual prayer of my life. To be honest, I feel like I don't even need to pray the prayer, because God seems to answer it in my life whether I pray it or not. That's because God never wants me to get comfortable in life.

Don't get me wrong; I love being comfortable. I think it comes naturally for most of us to take the easy road in life, play it safe, and never stretch out of our comfort zone. In fact, it seems like modern society is striving to eliminate risk and make comfort and safety the ultimate goal. Our families move into suburbs built for comfort, and we try to follow the American Dream. But note this: there's usually a big difference between the American Dream and God's dream for your life.

Although we naturally gravitate toward settling into our comfort zone of selfishness, that's where our souls begin to atrophy. That's where emptiness sets in. The reality is, if we're trying to have Christ *and* comfort, there's a good chance we're settling for a faith that's far less than what God wants us to have.

We would argue that the best measure of whether you have a firsthand faith in Christ is how much compassion you feel for people who are hurting—and what you're willing to do about it. Secondhand religion causes you to be absorbed in yourself, but firsthand faith moves you out of selfishness and into the lives of others.

> Although we naturally gravitate toward settling into our comfort zone of selfishness, that's where our souls begin to atrophy.

You were created to take great risks in faith and face great challenges, living a life of adventure. The rewards may not be as tangible as the ones you could acquire for yourself by pursuing a life of selfishness, but in their own way they're so much greater! As you're reading this chapter, keep asking yourself if you're ready for the adventure of taking part in the great work God is doing in the lives of the people near you and all over the world.

Oh Wow

Steve Jobs built the Apple corporation into one of the most valuable and innovative companies in the world. He was also one of the great communicators of our time. His speeches unveiling new Apple products were legendary. But he uttered his most profound and powerful words on the last day of his life.

His sister, Mona Simpson, who was at his side, said his last words were "Oh wow. Oh wow. Oh wow." A few hours later he passed away.

We don't know why Steve Jobs's last words were "Oh wow." We do believe, however, that most of us will have an "Oh wow" moment in the last minutes or hours of our lives on earth, when everything comes into brilliant focus, and we have total clarity on what really matters. We'll have an "Oh wow" moment because we'll realize completely that our time on earth is limited, and we'll wish we had spent more of our sacred seconds moving outside of ourselves and showing the love of Christ to others.

But here's the thing. We believe God wants us to have that "Oh wow" moment long before our last moments on earth. Why? So we have time to do something that will outlast our one and only life on this earth. The sooner we have that moment, the better. And if we can have it when we're young people making the transition from secondhand faith to firsthand faith, that's best.

One of the ways God gives us a wake-up call is by putting what we call a "divine disturbance" in our souls. A divine disturbance is any way that God shakes us out of our selfish complacency and into the lives of others. For you it may come as a message whispered into your spirit by God's Spirit, a troubling experience, a Scripture verse you can't get out of your head, or something else.

But it will always be God's way of saying, "It's time to wake up and join Me in the great things I'm doing in the world."

> A divine disturbance is any way that God shakes us out of our selfish complacency and into the lives of others.

God has given me (Josh) several divine disturbances to rock my world and shove me into His purpose for me. In fact, I had an earthquake of a divine disturbance the first time I went to Africa on a mission trip.

Our church has a ministry to young people in the Kware slum district of Nairobi, Kenya, and the first time I went, it changed my life and woke me up to what is happening in our world. As we drove into the slum, the smell of trash and sewage hit my nostrils. Then as we got out of the car and walked the narrow streets, we came across half-naked children running around, playing with an old tire and carrying younger siblings. Near the middle of the slum was a hill where I could see tiny huts patched together with dirt and old metal stretching out in every direction across the horizon.

The destitution I saw was appalling, yet what was more amazing was the absolute joy and purpose I saw in the Kenyan students we met. Many of them were my age, and they were constantly looking for ways to serve their community, whether it was providing dinner for a church member in need or helping the younger kids study for school. They were so sensitive to the hurt and suffering that surrounded them, and they took joy in being the hands and feet of Christ.

It sent a disturbing shock wave through my soul when I had to come to grips with the fact that every day I drink a five-dollar toffee nut latte while half the world lives on less than two dollars a day!

It was impossible to keep my heart from breaking the first time I came face to face with another human being in absolute poverty. To think of how the world, me included, could allow someone's suffering to go unnoticed for that long was genuinely disturbing.

Firsthand Disturbance

Jesus told a story that should send a shudder into our souls and divinely disturb us every time we read it. It's in Matthew 25, the story of how at the end of time the Master (God) will separate the sheep from the goats—that is, the righteous from the unrighteous.

The Master tells all those who love Him to come and take their inheritance, explaining:

> I was hungry and you fed me,
> I was thirsty and you gave me a drink,
> I was homeless and you gave me a room,

I was shivering and you gave me clothes,

I was sick and you stopped to visit,

I was in prison and you came to me.

(verses 35–36, MSG)

Then all the righteous respond to Him with a question of sheer surprise: "Master, what are you talking about? When did we ever see you hungry and feed you, thirsty and give you a drink? And when did we ever see you sick or in prison and come to you?" (verses 37–38, MSG).

After this the Master replies, "I'm telling the solemn truth: Whenever you did one of these things to someone overlooked or ignored, that was me—you did it to me" (verse 40, MSG).

What great news this is for the people who are faithfully serving God! In one sense the needy people of the world are Christ in disguise.

But there's another category of people who are facing God, and they get very different news.

The Master turns to the unrighteous and says that when He was hungry and thirsty and needy, they didn't care. Then come some of the most disturbing verses in all of Scripture:

Then those "goats" are going to say, "Master, what are you talking about? When did we ever see you hungry or thirsty or homeless or shivering or sick or in prison and didn't help?"

He will answer them, "I'm telling the solemn truth:

Whenever you failed to do one of these things to someone who was being overlooked or ignored, that was
me—you failed to do it to me."

Then those "goats" will be herded to their eternal
doom, but the "sheep" to their eternal reward." (verses
44–46, MSG)

Maybe you're thinking, *Wait a minute! I thought faith was
all about receiving grace and it didn't have anything to do with
works.*

That's right. The Bible tells us that salvation is not about
what we can do for God but about what God has done for us
through Christ (Ephesians 2:8–9). It's all undeserved grace.

Of course salvation is all about encountering God's grace.
But here Jesus is saying that if you have no compassion for
the least of these—the poorest, neediest, and most neglected
people in the world—then chances are, you have not encountered His firsthand grace. When you experience a firsthand faith with the Grace Giver, He changes you into a grace
giver yourself.

If you have no compassion for the poorest,
neediest, and most neglected people in the
world, then chances are, you have not
encountered God's grace.

More than three thousand verses in the Bible deal with compassion and justice for the poor. It's not a side item in the Bible. It's God's heart! He has a heart that is disturbed and broken when He sees the hurt and brokenness in our world.

Bob Pierce, the founder of World Vision, encountered the plight of orphans in Korea with the same kind of shock I encountered with the poor of Nairobi. Afterward, he wrote on the flyleaf of his Bible, "Let my heart be broken with the things that break the heart of God."

Let your heart and ours be broken in the same way.

SECONDHAND STATISTICS

We want to share with you some disturbing facts we once heard from Pastor Rick Warren.

- If you have food in your refrigerator, clothes on your back, a roof over your head, and a place to sleep, then you're better off than 75 percent of the world today.

- If you have any amount of money in a bank account or in your wallet, then you're better off than 92 percent of the world's population.

- If you've never experienced the pangs of starvation, then you are better off than the 500 million people who are experiencing starvation right now while you're reading this sentence.

These facts should disturb us. Usually, however, it takes

more than facts to disturb us enough to do something. I know it did for me (Ryan).

My mom has been leading our church's mission work in Haiti since the devastating earthquake of 2010. She told me the disturbing statistics that more than 300,000 people had lost their lives, that 1.3 million people were still living in tents a year after the quake, that 300,000 children were orphaned and had nowhere to go and no one looking out for them. I felt bad about it, but the statistics didn't mean much to me, to be honest. It wasn't until I experienced the situation firsthand that I became divinely and deeply disturbed.

Last year I accompanied my mom on one of her mission trips to Haiti. I was there mainly to film the work going on in order to encourage more people in the church to go on the continuous trips. After filming the clean-water system, school, and coffee ministry we had started, we took a trip out to a place that left me completely undone. It was the area where, right after the earthquake, the Haitians disposed of thousands of unidentified bodies before their decay could spread disease to the living.

We arrived at this massive grave site on the one-year anniversary of the earthquake. I started to film as thousands of people streamed by, going to what looks like the city dump to pay respects to their loved ones who died in the quake. But soon I had to put my camera down and turn it off as the enormity of their tragedy came over me like a wave. I watched as widows, orphans, and friends walked in solemn silence to pay their respects.

I had driven by this grave site several times since we'd arrived in the country, but I had never even noticed it. Yet now I understood. These weren't numbers in a textbook I could just glance over; these were broken people. It dawned on me that the faces in front of me had names and loved ones and real pain.

Thousands of people with tears in their eyes were going to what they assumed was where their loved ones' remains ended up—in a giant pit of dirt and trash. Suddenly all those statistics started exploding in my head: *300,000 people dead, 300,000 orphans, 1.3 million people in tents!* God disturbed me deeply as I moved from secondhand statistics to firsthand grief. These were no longer mere statistics but real people who had experienced pain I couldn't begin to comprehend.

God used that experience to move me out of my selfishness and into service. Now I'm committed to going back to Haiti and wherever else God takes me to make whatever difference I can in serving the poor and the powerless with the love of Christ.

From Disturbance to Doing Something

It is impossible to have a firsthand faith without acting upon the divine disturbance God puts on your heart. Sometimes that disturbance comes as a complete surprise.

One day my (Josh's) friend Logan, who is getting her master's degree at Belmont University, went with her class on a trip to Tennessee's death row. To say Logan was disturbed by what she saw would be an understatement. One inmate in particular had a profound impact on Logan. His name is RC.

For months Logan and RC wrote to each other. She learned that, in order to stay productive, he had begun making art and jewelry.[11] Beyond his passion to create, he actively represents the interests of other prisoners, and he hopes to start a program that would permit death-row prisoners to assist with suicide hotlines. His reasoning? "Who is better qualified to talk a person out of suicide than one who fights each day to live and, despite the lingering possibility of death, doesn't fall victim to despair?"

What disturbed Logan was not the issue of capital punishment; it was seeing another human being—someone with talents, fears, insecurities, and dreams—who was being ignored and unloved. Too often we see issues as black and white, wrong or right. Pro-life or pro-choice. For or against capital punishment. Pro-LGBT or against. Simplifying things in this way makes it easier to comprehend complicated issues...and sometimes to explain away the injustice we see in the world around us. Logan did not see things that way when it came to RC.

It's easy to have an opinion or believe in a cause, but we have to allow our hearts to be disturbed if we are going to act in love. Viewing injustice as a black-and-white issue is crippling to a first-hand faith. I'm not saying that we should ignore biblical principles or abandon our convictions. I'm advocating the opposite. We have to allow ourselves to be disturbed by the human experience. Jesus came to love, and we are called to do the same.

It's easy to have an opinion or believe in a cause, but we have to allow our hearts to be disturbed if we are going to act in love.

We are all imperfect. We all have made mistakes. But Jesus did not hang out with sinners and tax collectors to condemn them and judge them and point out their flaws; He did it because He cared and hurt deeply for them (Matthew 9:10–13). He wanted them to experience the love God had for them firsthand, so He met them where they were with conviction and love.

The needs of this world are endless. So whenever we feel a divine disturbance, it's essential that we respond with firsthand action. If we don't, it will quickly turn into secondhand bitterness, as I found out personally.

THE CHALLENGE

I (Josh) remember how, when I got into college, I became more and more frustrated with the worship music in church. (Not with the people leading worship but with the type of songs.) I began to complain to my roommates and friends about what I perceived as an oversimplification of our human struggle and God's answer to that struggle. I was feeling a divine disturbance that there should be new worship music from my generation that expressed a raw and real relationship with God.

After a while, however, I let my divine disturbance turn into bitterness that became a barrier between me and the Lord. Whenever I heard the songs in church, I would start to think about all the things I didn't like about them instead of thinking about the incredible God they glorified.

I had many conversations with my dad, voicing my frustration. "All these songs we sing are poorly written and incredibly simple!" I would say. "Doesn't God deserve the best of what we can create?"

Then one day Dad challenged me in a way I had not expected. "All right, Josh," he said. "Why don't you and your band mates lead worship one weekend a month and plan the Sunday night service? You're always saying that worship needs to be different and that we should try new things and write new songs, so God has obviously put that on your heart. I really believe this could be a great opportunity for the church."

Quickly I started back-pedaling. "Well, I don't know if that's really my calling or what I want to do with my life."

"That's fine!" my dad said. "It's just one weekend a month, and if you decide you don't want to do it after a weekend or two, you don't have to."

I had just been called out, and I was unprepared. It was easy to criticize and point at things I felt needed improvement, but it was something else entirely to take responsibility for addressing them.

I learned an important principle in all of this: when we feel uneasy about the way things are done or not done, we should view them for what they are—unmet needs.

> When we feel uneasy about the way things are done or not done, we should view them for what they are—unmet needs.

The world and unfortunately the church too are full of critics and people just waiting to cut others down. This is the opposite of what we are called to do. We are to "encourage one another and build each other up" (1 Thessalonians 5:11). Yes, there are times when we are called to accountability, and everything we do must be grounded in God's Word. But we must learn to recognize inaction.

James tells us that faith without works is dead (James 2:26). The most certain way to go back to living a secondhand faith is to refuse to act upon the Holy Spirit's movement in your heart, a divine disturbance.

When you do not respond to a divine disturbance of the Holy Spirit, you get bitter and you criticize. That helps no one. You are called to serve and to love with your actions (Galatians 5:13). More specifically, you hurt yourself. It becomes easy to think that you know how to do things better than the people God has appointed to be a part of your life. When you don't respond to a divine disturbance in your life, you become the greatest obstacle between an unbelieving world and a loving God—a judgmental Christian.

We are called to act in love, and the firsthand experience is an exciting, sometimes terrifying, journey that requires us to step out in faith and depend on the Lord and learn from His Word every day. That's exactly how it worked when I took up my dad's challenge to lead worship at Woodlands Church.

LEARNING TO RELY ON THE LORD

For a few months now, my friends and I (Josh) have been flying in from Nashville one weekend a month to lead worship at Woodlands Church, and it has forced me to rely on the Lord in ways I did not have to previously.

Before leading worship, I had been living in Nashville and had been writing and playing music without overt references to the Lord or a church setting. Frankly, I liked it. For me, it was a way of coming out from my parents' shadow. So I felt as if going back to my home church to lead worship would be a failure, saying that the music thing hadn't worked out for me and now I would just move back in with my parents and sing in church.

But responding to the divine disturbance the Lord placed on my heart regarding worship music has forced me to find my identity in Christ, not in the style or subject of the music I play. Confronting my insecurities about playing in church, because of how I felt about worship music and how I wanted others to view me, has been liberating because I have experienced how the Lord uses us when we simply respond to Him.

The incredible response we have received from playing once a month, and the conversations I have had with people after the services (mainly regarding the honesty in our songs and our testimony), have convinced me that God is using our small contribution to Woodlands Church to do some pretty cool things in people's lives. And that is incredibly rewarding and validating. Even better, it has become so much easier to acknowledge the Lord's role in what we are doing because I am constantly confronting my own insecurities and shortcomings and learning how to deal with them through His Word. It is beautiful to experience, even in small ways, how God makes His strength perfect in my weakness (2 Corinthians 12:9).

I still struggle every month and pray, "God, I've got nothing to write or sing about. What are we going to do?" But I am learning that anxiety is healthy, because when I recognize my imperfection, I look for inspiration from the Lord. The great artist Picasso said, "Inspiration exists. It just has to find us working." I love that quote because I am so lazy, but it really does apply to our relationship with the Lord.

I always pray for God to move and inspire me or solve my problems, but I hardly ever put forth the effort to pursue Him. I am discovering that responding to the divine disturbances God places on my heart forces me to search Him out. In my case, having a monthly deadline has actually been very freeing and has brought me closer to the Lord, not because I am leading worship in church, but because the deadlines force me to sit down and spend time with Him. That is a good thing, because church is pretty useless if the people who plan it are not actively seeking God's will. In the process of trying to be obedient, I grow closer to the Lord.

THE DAY OF RECKONING

What we have learned, and what Logan and so many others from our generation have learned, is that making a difference in the world has nothing to do with how talented you are or how much money you have. Your eternal footprint—the impact you make on this earth—will be determined by whether you respond to the calling of the Spirit of the Lord in your heart to love a broken world, to step into the gifts and passions the Lord has blessed you with to meet the needs that others overlook.

> Your eternal footprint will be determined by whether you respond to the calling of the Spirit to love a broken world.

Do you remember a board game called the Game of Life? As kids we played it a lot with our family. We'd each start off with a little plastic SUV and then put our little plastic pink and blue pegs in our cars. As we went along in the game, we had to make some decisions—things like *Will I get married or not? Will*

I have a career or not? At the end we came to a square called the "Day of Reckoning," where we had to account for our debts and the decisions we'd made during the game.

Well, the truth is that there really will be a day of reckoning. The Bible says it is the day when all of us—everyone who has ever lived—will stand before God and give an account for how we spent our lives. That's what the parable of the sheep and the goats in Matthew 25 is all about. And we think there are two things God will ask us on that day.

First of all, He's going to ask us, "What did you do with My Son, Jesus Christ? Did you have a firsthand faith in Him?"

And the second question will be "What did you do with the divine disturbances I put in your soul? Your time, talents, treasure—I gave them all to you. Now, what did you do with them in the areas where I was trying to get you involved?"

Step out in firsthand faith, and do something for someone else, and leave the results to God. He can do extraordinary things through ordinary and imperfect people like you and like us. We're confident of one thing: whenever you stand for the poor and powerless, God stands with you!

Making It Real

Other Voices

For the past two years, I've been a part of a new outreach started by my church's youth group. It's called Beyond Our Walls, and it's a way for preteens and teens to minister to and help others—without the goal being to bring people to church or to get something out of it ourselves. I've organized a pro-life awareness campaign and a pregnancy crisis center donation drive. I've also volunteered in our church's ministries, helping at the nursing home and feeding the homeless. Through BOW I learned both how to be a leader and how to be one of the more overlooked but still important people in the background. I've also learned how to make my faith real outside my church, in my own life—my "real life." —*Emily from Warner Robins, Georgia*

Being involved with a ministry to help homeless women and children has helped me mature in my faith to God. When I am with the people there, I try to see Jesus in them because I believe that when we help a homeless person, it is like we are helping Jesus (Matthew 25:34–40). Serving with this ministry has given me a passion for the poor, which has enabled me to try to be a voice for them within my denomination. —*Jill from Grayson, Georgia*

When I was in college, I got involved with a group of students who went down to Philadelphia and cleaned out Tent City as the residents sought a warmer location to live in for the winter. They had discovered an unused Catholic church. So we helped them get their stuff and helped them clean up everything so they could move in. On the same day a friend and I helped a guy go buy milk.

As I reached out to these folks, I heard their stories. I heard the faith they held even as they struggled to live. This event planted in me a vision to reach my neighbors and discover the full meaning of 1 John 3:16–18, where John talks about imitating Christ's love and giving sacrificially so that others might know Christ. —*Joel from Bernville, Pennsylvania*

God has shown me the need for helping others as part of growing our faith. If I'm still so focused on me and my wants and desires after being a Christian for five years, I may not be following Him. As I mature in my walk with Christ, He switches my desires and my heart with His desires and heart, and the first thing that happens is that He gives me a genuine love for others, because His heart is for others to come to know Him. —*Nydia from Beaumont, Texas*

Think About It

1. Has God ever challenged you to step out of your comfort zone to help the needy? If so, what was it like?

2. How do you feel about spending time with people who are poor and disadvantaged? Or with people who are from a different culture and faith than yours? If you're hesitant about being with them, what specifically is holding you back?

3. Is there anything you've been complaining about that might indicate an area where you need to stop complaining and start doing something constructive? What's your first step?

4. How do you think it would affect your faith if you started doing challenging things to help some of the world's needy?

Might Try This

● **Watch the film *Picture Perfect*.**

Ryan has created a short film called *Picture Perfect,* which talks about how we're all surrounded by people in need. Watch it online by going to FirsthandBook.com/Picture, and think about the needy people in your circle of experience that God might be calling you to help.

● Read a biography.

There are lots of great books, some movies, and of course online profiles that tell about great figures in the history of Christian missions and outreach. Check out at least one person's story—it will inspire you! Below are a few of the many biographies and autobiographies available in book form:

- *George Müller of Bristol* by A. T. Pierson
- *The Life and Diary of David Brainerd,* edited by Jonathan Edwards
- *Mary Slessor: Forward into Calabar* or *C. T. Studd: No Retreat,* both by Janet and Geoff Benge
- *To the Golden Shore: The Life of Adoniram Judson* by Courtney Anderson
- *Faithful Witness: The Life and Mission of William Carey* by Timothy George

● Learn Jesus's outreach guidelines.

Read Luke 10:1–24, which is the story of Jesus sending out a bunch of ordinary people like you and like us to spread His kingdom. What do you learn from it about the role of prayer? the risks involved? having trust in God? the reactions of other people? the effects of all this in the spiritual realm?

● Go!

Check with your church or a parachurch ministry about opportunities for doing outreach or mission work, whether it's near or far from where you live. Then pick something, sign up, and go do it!

Or if you're the entrepreneurial sort, start your own cause, and enlist others to help you carry it out.

● **Pray.**

Ask God to disturb your soul about something He wants you to do—and to give you the courage to respond to that disturbance. In addition, ask Him to show you more about who He is and who you are as His child as you follow through in obedience.

You might need to pray about all this, not just once, but for a while.

8

Firsthand Community

A Faith That Forms a Movement

What should young people do with
their lives today? Many things,
obviously. But the most daring thing
is to create stable communities.

—Kurt Vonnegut

What we do in life echoes in eternity.

—Maximus, gladiator

We started this book by telling how, as two "good church kids," we began to doubt everything we'd learned about God and the right way to live. We talked about how it felt like we were crossing a bridge that ended halfway across the river. Ahead—only fog. Our childhood faith wasn't able to stretch all the way into the adult lives that lay before us. So what were we going to do? It was a confusing and disturbing time—and, honestly, a potentially dangerous one.

Well, we're pleased to be able to say that the bridge makes it all the way across now. After some time spent lost in the swirling mists, we each found a firsthand faith of our own that we really believe, that in fact we're prepared to stake everything we have on. Not that we don't still have questions and failures, of course. Lots of them! But it's no longer a question of whether we're going on in life with Christ or not. We belong to Him from now on, whatever may come. And we're pumped about the adventure He has in store for us!

How about you?

Our hope is that, with the help of the chapters you've been

through, you're on your way to forming a faith that is unique and every bit your own. A faith that isn't cookie-cutter religion but a relationship that is real, alive, and growing…even if it is messy sometimes.

We expect by this point you've come to agree with us that a sense of emptiness is often what brings us back to God—because you've felt that emptiness too. We hope you've learned to equate truth with freedom and to submit to the remodeling process God wants to carry out in your life. We have little doubt that it came as a relief to you to hear that you don't have to live by a checklist of dos and don'ts in place of a relationship with Christ. We're sure it was encouraging to discover that you don't have to feel insecure about your doubts and fears but instead can work through them to develop a faith that's real. And we hope, too, that you're excited about the possibility that God will call you to act on your firsthand faith and do something that really matters in this hurting world.

But there's one more thing we need to say to you.

You can't do this alone.

We're not talking about living out your faith with God at your side. It should go without saying that your faith is a gift from God and that you can't act on it apart from Him. No, we're talking about living out a real faith in Jesus *with other people.* This is where it all starts to seem more doable, doesn't it? And where it becomes more fun.

Throughout this book we've mentioned being in community

with others. Ways that the two of us have encouraged each other. Times when our parents helped us through the fog of our faith crises. Points where we depended on friends and mentors to listen to our thoughts and hold us accountable for the kind of lives we intended to live. We didn't get across the bridge alone. We came in a group.

We want you to have that kind of help along the way too.

We have a vision of young people like you and like us joining with others who desire a firsthand faith. These others might be young adults themselves, or they might be older mentors with more wisdom and experience to share. Our hope is that you find your firsthand community in friendships, as part of your local church, in a small group, and maybe even in a community you start yourself. The point is, you're not alone in figuring out and living out a mature faith in Jesus.

> We have a vision of young people joining with others who desire a firsthand faith.

THE FIRST FIRSTHAND COMMUNITY

We've all taken a pebble and tossed it into a glassy-calm pond, then watched as the ripples spread wider and wider across the pond. Christianity has a ripple effect—the actions of Jesus and His early followers spread out through time until they formed the church and brought a Christian influence to the world we know today. Let us take you to the story found in Matthew 14 to show you one way those ripples got started.

Jesus, having become worn-out from healing the sick and ministering to many, took His twelve disciples to a remote region to get away from the crowds. But the crowds followed Him anyway. Christ had compassion on them and began to teach. By the end of the day, everyone was tired and hungry, and this led to an interesting exchange between Jesus and His disciples.

> The disciples came to [Jesus] and said, "This is a remote place, and it's already getting late. Send the crowds away, so they can go to the villages and buy themselves some food."
>
> Jesus replied, "They do not need to go away. You give them something to eat." (verses 15–16)

This wasn't the response the disciples were hoping for or expecting. *Us feed the people?* they must have been thinking. *Are You kidding, Jesus? Thousands of people here, and You think we have the means to feed them?*

If we ever take the time to contemplate what it would look like for us to help others fill their spiritual emptiness with Jesus, we might easily react as the disciples did. *No way, Jesus. That's way too big a job for me.*

The disciples were determined to get out of this one. They pointed out that they'd already looked around and that the only resources they had to work with were a measly five loaves of bread and two fish.

"Bring them here to me," Jesus said. Then He did something strange and wonderful.

> He directed the people to sit down on the grass. Taking the five loaves and the two fish and looking up to heaven, he gave thanks and broke the loaves. Then he gave them to the disciples, and the disciples gave them to the people. They all ate and were satisfied, and the disciples picked up twelve basketfuls of broken pieces that were left over. The number of those who ate was about five thousand men, besides women and children. (verses 18–21)

Five loaves and two fish turned into more food than you've ever seen at the biggest wedding banquet or church potluck you've ever been to!

This wasn't Jesus's way of saying to the disciples, "You losers! I've got so much more going on than you." No, we think He was saying, "This is the kind of thing you guys can do with God. You're a part of something big here. So no more small-minded thinking, please."

Really, in a sense, the disciples themselves *were* the five loaves and two fish. They were a group of ordinary guys, a resource of limited potential from all appearances. But they were the means Jesus had chosen to transmit His message to the whole world after

He was gone. God was able to miraculously multiply their effectiveness in ministering to the spiritually hungry of the world.

So when we talk about your need to be a part of a firsthand community, we're not suggesting anything new. We're actually following the pattern that Jesus first established with the disciples. A group of people who aren't perfect but who are committed to helping each other know and serve Jesus can live out a faith that is more powerful than they could have ever imagined, and it happens through the amazing power of Christ. This really works. Throughout history, whenever the church of Jesus Christ has made an important advance, this is how it has happened.

> A group of people who aren't perfect but who are committed to helping each other know and serve Jesus can live out a faith that is more powerful than they could have ever imagined.

It's probably true, in fact, that none of the great movements of history was begun by one man or one woman alone. The truly great movements began with small but dedicated groups of people. We love this story of Jesus feeding the five thousand because it gives us a vivid picture of how a firsthand community of faithful Christ followers can gain momentum and become a movement.

The community of Christians takes many forms. But there is one we cannot afford to neglect: the local church.

Church: The Hope of the World

When we set out to discover our own firsthand faith, we were disillusioned with church. We had seen how imperfect the church could be, and we were certain that church was the problem. Coming full circle with our firsthand faith, we now realize that church was not the problem. The problem was our view and definition of church itself.

It took us a long time to understand that church wasn't a building or a pastor or a sermon series. It's easy to point out everything wrong with the church when you stand outside it and approach it with a consumer mentality. We thought the church had given us a secondhand faith, when in reality we had chosen to avoid a firsthand relationship with the community of Christ followers we claimed to care about.

Paul wrote this to the followers of Christ in Corinth: "You are Christ's body—that's who you are! You must never forget this. Only as you accept your part of that body does your 'part' mean anything" (1 Corinthians 12:27, MSG).

You are part of the body of Christ. *You* are the church. The amazing truth is that you are a member of the most powerful, intimate, and meaningful community in history! God didn't design you for a secondhand relationship wasted on the sidelines of life. He wants you to experience deep and rich community in His body!

Are you a firsthand member of your local church? Or are

you sitting on the sidelines? The church is messy and imperfect because it is made up of broken and imperfect people. Are you sitting on the sidelines because the people in your church are imperfect or "just not like you"? Paul went on to explain in 1 Corinthians that Christ designed the church to be made up of many different people with unique characteristics and talents.

God designed you to be in community with your local church. He designed you to have firsthand relationships not only with Him but also with the people in your church. You can come up with plenty of excuses not to get involved or reasons that your church has it wrong, but when was the last time you looked inside yourself and really searched your own heart for issues? It took us a long time to understand that the source of our secondhand faith wasn't in the church; it was in our own hearts.

> You can come up with plenty of reasons that your church has it wrong, but when was the last time you searched your own heart for issues?

It's impossible to live a completely firsthand faith without living out your faith in the community of Christ followers God has placed around you. And you need every bit of support you can get to live out a firsthand faith in this spiritually dangerous world.

Beware the Second-Handers

In the novel *The Fountainhead,* the protagonist is an architect named Howard Roark. At one point he explains to a friend that he is committed to creating work that will reflect what he believes. He complains, though, that he is surrounded by people who "don't ask: 'Is this true?' "

> They ask: "Is this what others think is true?" Not to
> judge, but to repeat. Not to do, but to give the impression
> of doing. Not creation, but show.

Roark's friend then asks him why he has told him all this, and Roark replies, "[Because] you weren't born to be a second-hander."[12]

We wouldn't endorse everything in the philosophy behind this novel. But this statement has something to say to every one of us. *You weren't born to be a second-hander.*

And there's more. You won't get anywhere with a firsthand faith if you surround yourself with second-handers. You have to find others who share at least some of your passion to bring the real you to the real Jesus and see what happens.

We wish we could tell you that you will always be encouraged by people who recognize your firsthand faith. But the truth is that the world is filled with second-handers. Some second-handers will simply ignore you, but more will actually see your firsthand faith as a threat.

We've been living so long in a society that says that anything goes, that there are many roads to happiness, that complacency is the goal. Anyone who challenges those notions will naturally be seen as an enemy. If you argue that a personal and firsthand faith with your Creator is not only possible but is truly the best way to live, then be prepared to be attacked. If you start living out a firsthand faith in the world around you, then expect to be criticized and looked down upon by the rest of the world.

> If you don't have the right kind of community to support you through good times and bad, you will be taken out of the game by second-handers eager to bring down anyone who stands apart from the crowd.

You weren't born to be a second-hander. You were designed to live out a firsthand faith that is vibrant and fulfilling. But the firsthand life is not meant to be lived alone. When you try to live out a firsthand faith on your own, you are bound to fail. You can set out with the best intentions, but if you don't have a community—the right kind of community—around you to support you through good times and bad, you will be taken out of the game by second-handers eager to bring down anyone who stands apart from the crowd.

Your People

You will never be able to fully understand what a firsthand faith looks like until you are living in community. What we're talking about is a community of Christians who know they have a firsthand connection with Christ and are passionate about making the world a better place, one that reflects that firsthand relationship in all its glory.

A woman named Jamie from Carlsbad, California, discovered the importance of having a community of such believers around her. For her, a big issue was dealing with sin.

She said, "Your young adult years are the time of your life when you go through the most temptation. It was having a strong fellowship with those who believed like me that kept me from straying too far."

Then Jamie gave an example from the summer she was eighteen.

"I worked at a beach and got to hanging out with some of the kids at the beach. I started drinking and partying with them. It was so bad that, after working a Sunday afternoon, I partied with them and then showed up at church drunk. My true friends at church talked with me and prayed with me and showed me that I had everything I needed with them. I could be myself, not someone I wasn't."

A firsthand community doesn't have to be a bunch of young people. Ashton, a twenty-eight-year-old from Warrenton, Missouri, has discovered the value of intergenerational Christian community—something we've discovered too.

"Without some of my closest friends," Ashton says, "I would wonder, *Am I the only one struggling with this?* I need people in my life who share the same struggles in this life, to encourage me to make it." Like Jamie, Ashton realized early on the importance of having friends who genuinely cared about him on a deeper level.

But Ashton also wants mentors. He says, "As I grow older, I am also discovering my need for someone who has already made it through this stage or this battle who can cheer me on with experience."

You can try to live out a firsthand faith on your own for as long as you want, but until you live out that faith in a community, you will never realize your full potential in Christ.

There are lots of ways of getting involved with and building firsthand community. What it looks like might not even matter so much. What matters is that you *have* such a community. In fact, we're prepared to make this claim: you can try to live out a firsthand faith on your own for as long as you want, but until you live out that faith in a community, you will never realize your full potential in Christ.

FIRSTHAND GENERATION

One author called our generation "Generation Ex-Christian."[13] He cites the same kind of statistics as we referred to in chapter 1 about the number of young people who are leaving church or disassociating themselves from Christianity entirely. But really, Generation Ex-Christian? The stats may say that, but the faith inside us says there's a different possibility entirely.

And we're not the only ones holding out hope for something better. Christian Smith, a researcher looking at a massive study of the religious and spiritual lives of what he calls "emerging adults" (people between the ages of eighteen and twenty-three), weighed in on whether the young adult years are really what many people think—a black hole that inevitably sucks the faith out of people.

> Certain social and cultural forces at work during emerging adulthood…exert influences something like the powerful gravitational field of a black hole, which seems almost inexorably to pull everything that comes close

enough to it into its consuming darkness. But we have also learned that those forces are not so strong that they always engulf all of the visible "light" of religion among youth simply because their lives have passed the demographic "event horizon" from the teenage years into emerging adulthood.[14]

It's possible that the black hole will claim many victims. More to the point, it's possible the black hole will claim *you* if you choose to just let your secondhand faith go cold without struggling your way to a firsthand faith that replaces it. But we agree with Smith. Our generation is not doomed to be known to history as Generation Ex-Christian. We think, in fact, that it has the potential to be the Firsthand Generation—a generation in which huge numbers refuse to accept hand-me-down religion and instead hold out for the real thing.

Not so sure that's possible? Stop for a moment to think about the time in which we live and the unique potential our generation has.

Matthew 24:14 says, "This gospel of the kingdom will be preached in the whole world as a testimony to all nations, and then the end will come." There won't be a need for any more generations to be added to the long chain of humankind, because the purpose of spreading the story of Jesus to all peoples will be achieved.

Through technology and billions of interconnected relationships, it is possible that within our lifetime Jesus Christ could be known by every person on earth. Our generation is the first to see the Internet reach every corner of the globe, cell phones in almost everyone's hands, and constant communication across every nation.

The same forces at work in the early church are being amplified in our world today: the importance of connectedness, the role of community, the multiplying effect of God through the power of the gospel. Jesus's original twelve disciples didn't have the Web or smart phones, but if they had, don't you think they would have immediately seen the potential of these tools?

Just think, if our generation began working together to live out a firsthand faith daily, we could literally change the world. We're not talking about taking over an organization or ruling with selfish pride. We're talking about a firsthand generation that cares more about serving others than being served. A firsthand generation that is driven by the unique passions God has given them and doesn't compromise in the face of adversity.

If our generation began working together to live out a firsthand faith daily, we could literally change the world.

As a Christian, you are part of a movement that will outlast you, and you are part of the Firsthand Generation. As communities of believers rise up, we will gain momentum and create a movement that is stronger than anything we could ever accomplish on our own. Perhaps God is calling you to gather people and become a leader in the Firsthand Generation. Take up the challenge.

Never forget: you were not meant to be a second-hander. You have begun living out a firsthand faith that is authentic and vibrant, and it is time to take that faith into the world. Get with some other like-minded people, and do it *together*.

Making It Real

Other Voices

In college I had friends I could tell my darkest thoughts and deeds to, and they would uphold me in prayer and keep me accountable. But they weren't just accountability partners. I think the greatest gift I got from other people was when they shared where they saw God's work in my heart and His hand on my life. I am who I am because people spoke life into me. —*James from Blaine, Washington*

Very few of my friends are religious at all. The few that are, however, are like family. There is a closeness between us that the others cannot touch, because we know we are connected as brothers and sisters of Christ.

I always felt like I should hide my faith since I was the odd one out. Now I know that I should be proud of what I believe in and never be ashamed. My spiritual friends have helped me mature spiritually and be proud of my faith. —*Hannah from White River Junction, Vermont*

In my later teen years, I had a couple of close friends. One of them was a brand-new Christian. I had grown accustomed to playing a part to please my parents and others in the church. But my friend was accustomed to simply being honest. He would ask pointed questions, and it was all I could do to keep up with his growth. Of course, the benefit ended up being my own growth. —*Rick from Winona Lake, Indiana*

In my early twenties I had a wonderful mentor who was a Christian woman in her forties. Although we aren't able to spend much time together anymore, her words of wisdom stick with me even now. She was able to impart wisdom to me that I couldn't have gained any other way. —*Amy from Greensboro, North Carolina*

Think About It

1. How has your perspective on your personal faith in God changed since you started reading this book? What do you still need to make it your own—firsthand?

2. How have honest, genuine Christians helped your faith grow recently?

3. On a scale from one to ten (one meaning "really isolated" and ten meaning "really connected"), how connected to the Christian community have you been feeling lately?

4. What is your current church involvement like? What kind of church involvement do you think God would want you to have at this point in your life?

5. What will you do to find a firsthand community? What are some excuses you've been using to avoid authentic community?

Might Try This

● **Form a firsthand community of your own.**

Think about people you know who are serious about getting real in their faith in Jesus. Which ones could you approach about spending time together to encourage and support each other? What might a productive community with these people look like? Do you want to ask an older person to mentor you for a time? Do you want to start a small group that meets regularly?

Visit FirsthandBook.com/Community to find resources and learn about the Firsthand Small Group Curriculum, which includes relevant videos and tools from Ryan and Josh.

● **Reevaluate your church involvement.**

What's your attitude toward church? How regularly do you attend services? How do you contribute to what is going on? How can you be both a better "giver" and a better "taker" at church? Talk with a pastor to figure out where you can plug into your church most effectively.

● **Study the original firsthand community.**

Spend some time browsing through the Gospels and Acts to see how the disciples formed a group, grew together, and operated together in ministry. As you do so, think about what you can learn from their example for your own firsthand community.

Here are some key events to look at:

- Joining the group (Mark 1:14–20; 2:13–17; 3:13–19)
- Getting to a firsthand faith (Mark 8:27–30)
- Going on a short-term mission trip (Matthew 10)
- Seeing Jesus together in a new way (Luke 9:28–36)
- Failing together (Luke 9:37–45; 22:24–30)
- Arguing (Luke 9:46–50)
- Experiencing God's power in their midst (Acts 2:1–13)
- Doing greater things than they could have imagined (Acts 2:14–41; 3:1–4:31)
- Forming a transformational community life (Acts 2:42–47; 4:32–37)
- Mentoring others (Acts 9:26–28)

● **Pray.**

Here's our firsthand prayer that may help guide you as you try to live out a firsthand faith in authentic community:

> God, You know I'm not perfect. I bring all that I am to You. Use my gifts, my passions, and my heart to glorify You. When there is less of me, I know there will be more of You. Challenge me to always keep a firsthand relationship with You. Strengthen the firsthand community You've placed me in, and teach us to be Your hands and feet to this broken world. Thank You for never leaving me and constantly loving me no matter what. Amen.

Notes

1. David Kinnaman with Aly Hawkins, *You Lost Me: Why Young Christians Are Leaving Church…and Rethinking Faith* (Grand Rapids, MI: Baker, 2011), 22.

2. Jodi Fisler et al., "Keeping (or Losing) the Faith: Reflections on Spiritual Struggles and Their Resolution by College Seniors," *College Student Affairs Journal* 27, no. 2 (Spring 2009): 265.

3. "Most Twentysomethings Put Christianity on the Shelf Following Spiritually Active Teen Years," Barna Group, September 11, 2006, www.barna.org/barna-update/article /16-teensnext-gen/147-most-twentysomethings-put -christianity-on-the-shelf-following-spiritually-active -teen-years.

4. Robert P. Jones, Daniel Cox, and Thomas Banchoff, "A Generation in Transition: Religion, Values, and Politics Among College-Age Millennials—Findings from the 2012 Millennial Values Survey" (study performed by the Public Religion Research Institute Inc., and Georgetown University's Berkley Center for Religion, Peace, and World Affairs, April 2012), 7–8, http://publicreligion .org/site/wp-content/uploads/2012/04/Millennials -Survey-Report.pdf.

5. Cited in Mark D. Regnerus and Jeremy E. Uecker, "How Corrosive Is College to Religious Faith and Practice?" Social Science Research Council, February 5, 2007, http://religion.ssrc.org/reforum/Regnerus_Uecker.pdf. These numbers are corroborated by Rainer Research, which shows that 70 percent of youth (both college students and those who haven't attended college) leave church between the ages of eighteen and twenty-two. Thomas S. Rainer and Sam S. Rainer III, *Essential Church? Reclaiming a Generation of Dropouts* (Nashville: B&H, 2008), 3.

6. George Barna, *Maximum Faith: Live Like Jesus: Experience Genuine Transformation* (Carol Stream, IL: Tyndale, 2012), 157.

7. "Are Students Losing Their Religion on Campus?" ABC *Good Morning America,* December 6, 2005, http://abcnews.go.com/GMA/story?id=1375842&page=1#.UEKL4Y7CG22.

8. Frederick Buechner, *Telling Secrets* (New York: Harper-Collins, 1991), 2–3.

9. C. S. Lewis, *Mere Christianity* (New York: Harper-Collins, 2001), 205.

10. Oswald Chambers, "The Patience of Faith," *My Utmost for His Highest* (Uhrichsville, OH: Barbour, 2000), May 8 reading.

11. Logan now helps RC sell his products online—see etsy.com/shop/DeathRowArt. All proceeds go toward supplies for RC to make more of his products.

12. Ayn Rand, *The Fountainhead* (1943; reprint, New York: Plume, 1994), 634.

13. Drew Dyck, *Generation Ex-Christian: Why Young Adults Are Leaving the Faith…and How to Bring Them Back* (Chicago: Moody, 2010).

14. Christian Smith with Patricia Snell, *Souls in Transition: The Religious and Spiritual Lives of Emerging Adults* (New York: Oxford University Press, 2009), 282.

Acknowledgments

Thank you, Mom and Dad, for challenging us to discover our own firsthand faith.

Thank you, Sarah, for all the encouragement and patience you had with me (Ryan) throughout the entire process.

Thanks, Megan and Steven, for being the most loving and amazing siblings we could ever ask for.

We're thankful for our good friends Dave, Brandon, Joe, Spence, Calvin, Mike, Jon, Matt, Kyle, Chris, and Jon Mike. You guys challenged us to be real and were always there for us.

We're grateful for the team at WaterBrook Multnomah, including Dave Kopp, Ken Petersen, and Carie Freimuth. You were with us every step of the way and never gave up on us.

We're thankful for Tom Winters, who believed in us from the beginning and worked hard to get the book published.

We've been blessed to have so much help from the staff and members of Woodlands Church.

Thank you, reader, for reading this book and believing that a firsthand faith can change you from the inside out.

Most important, we want to acknowledge God's work and blessing in our lives. We don't deserve the opportunity to write a book or share our beliefs, but God gave it to us anyway.

About the Authors

Ryan Shook is a filmmaker and blogger whose short films are broadcast internationally and used at churches nationwide. A graduate of Baylor University, Ryan currently lives with his wife, Sarah, in Los Angeles. **Josh Shook** is a musician and recent graduate of Belmont University. Josh writes and produces music and currently resides in Nashville. Ryan and Josh are the sons of best-selling authors Kerry and Chris Shook, founders of Woodlands Church, near Houston.

FIRSTHANDBOOK.COM

Visit the website to learn more
about the Firsthand Experience,
watch the short films and
join the firsthand community.

/FIRSTHANDBOOK